Getting Done What Needs Doing

Dr. Lee Ann B. Marino, Ph.D., D.Min., D.D.

THE FUNCTIONS OF
THE CHURCH

Getting Done What Needs Doing

THE FUNCTIONS OF THE CHURCH

Dr. Lee Ann B. Marino, Ph.D., D.Min., D.D.

Published by:
Righteous Pen Publications
www.righteouspenpublications.com

Unless otherwise noted, Scriptures taken from the Holy Bible,
Authorized King James Version,
Public Domain.

Complete Scripture Copyright Reference List can be found on the preceding pages.

ISBN: 1940197287
13-Digit: 978-1-940197-28-9

Printed in the United States of America.

Scripture Copyright Reference List

Table Of Contents

Acknowledgements

I cannot publish this book without thanking the many people who have listened to me prattle on endlessly about functions over the past year. As I was processing the concept of the function and exploring more about what they are and how they work, I must pay tribute to the people who listened, asked questions, and even objected at times, because that made me go look the issues up and come up with better answers. As simple as a subject as this seemed to be when I started, I must admit that studying the functions in depth and developing this theory stretched my mind and made me explore many themes in the Bible I expected to be far more common than they are. I am truly indebted to each and every person who listened, made me think, made me stretch, and made me formulate that much more on this particular topic.

I am also very grateful to the handful of individuals who have long come and gone in my life who were highly instrumental in the formulation of my teaching as pertains to the functions of the church. Even though we might be separated by the miles and our ministry work has taken us in different directions, I am grateful for every person who helped me develop this teaching, past and present. May God bless each and every one of us as we move toward a more profound sense of unity in the Body of Christ.

Introduction

I have spent the past eight or so years of my life actively involved in the five-fold ministry in the office of the apostle. Prior to this time, we didn't talk about the five-fold ministry, but we did, on occasion, talk about some of the spiritual gifts. What we never talked about back then and still do not talk about in the way we should now are things that are on the "fringes" of spiritual gifts, in that they are never mentioned as being them, but are things that help the church to operate and help the church to function as a body. These works seemed to be all over the place: everything from visionaries to dream interpreters to writers and church mothers, impacting personal lives as well as benefiting the body of believers as a whole. Nowhere does the Bible indicate those who operate these works have to be leaders, although some do seem to take on a leadership role when operating the work. There isn't much on training for these works, they seem a lot of the time to be works that people do as needed, and they are often not particularly glamorous, and highly overlooked and underappreciated.

Because we never mentioned these things and we never discussed them or were taught about them back in the day, I didn't think much about them, myself. I might have seen mention to these different assorted works in the Bible, but I didn't take them beyond those immediate experiences. This seems odd to me now, especially because I have operated several of these works over the many years I have been a believer (at the time of this writing, over eighteen years). They were things I did, without much thinking, without any understanding, and just did them because they were needed at that time and God gave me the ability to do them.

As I was preparing my book, *Awakening Christian Ministry: The Call To Serve Others As We Serve Jesus Christ,* for publication last year, I became keenly aware of these "little things" that are neither offices nor gifts nor appointments that do not fit into any of the categories we often teach and preach about when it comes to gifts and leadership. They are things that so many people do, every day, with no name or identity. As I started to group these various things together, I categorized these different works as the functions of the church. I have so designated them as functions because they are things that help the body of believers and the church as a whole to function. They are not spiritual gifts, nor offices, nor appointments, but are things that God gives to His people in order to help us understand deeper spiritual things and meet every need according to His riches and glory in Christ Jesus. They are just as important, and just as needed, because they fill in and explain many gaps in our spiritual understanding and perspective. These functions are the things that make sure every need is met, even those that leadership are unable to meet due to the excessive demands of spiritual leadership, and those that are not met through spiritual gifts.

In recognizing there is little to no training available for the functions of the church (and those trainings that do exist are often incomplete or in error), I prayed about adding a functions training to the education and assignments we already do offer. In learning about the functions, we can understand better about the different spiritual needs and development we all have as believers. This study exists, in the same fashion as my earlier study on the five-fold ministry, to see where we best fit in as we experience and understand the role of the functions in our spiritual lives.

This book is formatted in a similar style to my book, *Awakening Christian Ministry: The Call To Serve Others As We Serve*

Jesus Christ, which covers the entire expanse of Christian ministry. Chapters 2-12 begin with a Bible study format, looking at the subject at hand from the Scriptures. We look at one primary verse, examining the Hebrew or Greek present, and then contrast the key verse in several different translations to capture the essence of what is being taught. We then look at the teaching in-depth, we look at people in history who fulfilled the function at hand, and answer questions and answers about that specific function. At the end of each of these chapters, you will find study and discussion questions, designed to help facilitate study and discussion about the function at hand.

The last chapter of the book discusses the specific situation of when an office or appointment becomes a function and the ways that the functions enhance the five-fold ministry. This may sound strange, but what we will be discussing here relates to situations that arise when a minister finds themselves without the assistance of others in the five-fold ministry and must complete the work of another ministry office. While they might be performing a work out of necessity for a period of time, they are not, in actuality, called to two or more offices. The work of the functions helps clarify the confusion many have on this topic and explains it in a way that is easily understandable.

In looking at the functions, I pray that this study will help expand your own Bible understanding and your own position in the Kingdom, sparking interest and excitement as we all work to get done the things that need doing in the Kingdom of God.

One ● ALL ABOUT FUNCTIONS

Whatever happens, conduct yourselves in a manner worthy of the Gospel of Christ.
Then, whether I come and see you or only hear about you in my absence, I will know
that you stand firm in one Spirit, contending as one man for the faith of the Gospel.
- Philippians 1:27 (NIV)

HAVE you ever tried to get something to work right, but it just seemed like there were so many gaps in the process, getting it to work was Impossible? Even though there might have been leadership in place and people to help the leaders, it seemed like there were many little things that seemed to come up that the leaders did not have the time to address and the helpers did not have the ability to address. In this instance, what happened? Most likely someone who was not specifically appointed to lead or to help stepped up and filled in that gap. Even if they were people appointed for another project, they were not individuals who were specifically there to help out on this one. They stepped in, addressed the need as best as they could, and then they resumed their regular position as pertained to the project.

This is how the functions of the church work. In the introduction of this book, I spoke about the things we are going to be looking at in this particular set of studies, and those things are called functions. There are eleven functions in the church, each one bringing with it a unique purpose and a unique set of operations to make sure every need within the church is met. There are all sorts of circumstances where these functions may become relevant and materialize, but each and every one of those situations represents a "gap," ones that are not answered by the stipulations of an office, or an appointment, or a spiritual gift.

WHAT ARE FUNCTIONS?

Functions are a unique classification of works that help to get things done. The functions are a part of the "helps ministries" of the church in that they are things that help assist the movement, growth, and maintenance of the church on a regular and especially an interpersonal basis. They are ways that every single one of us can participate by offering these works to one another within the Body of Christ. Those who operate in the functions do not need to be a part of the five-fold nor the appointments (although they can be and many of our Biblical examples were), and anyone can be a part of this essential functional work of the church as a body. Functions give the church a uniquely personal touch, because they prove that God cares about our every spiritual expression and makes sure we completely understand and hear from Him in every essential aspect of our lives. They are a type of work that we know enough about based on Bible examples and experiences (even though they are all not mentioned by name in the Bible) to specify them under this heading and examine more about them and how they operate.

The functions are unique because they show us the unique and essential connection between personal need and church life. We are all called to be a part of the church and to be connected to the church in some way, whether our connection to the church is primary universal (as within the context of some church offices) or primary local (as in the context of other forms of leadership and laity). The functions prove to us that God is interested in each and every one of us as individual people, not just as the concept of a larger church body or a corporate entity. While there is no question and no doubt that the church needs structure and it needs to follow the laws of the land wherever contained, the church is about more than administration, legalities, rites, sermons, weekly meetings, and Bible studies. The church is more than just a distant, detached building in this world; it is the living organism, made up of people who have different gifts, different callings, and come from different backgrounds. The functions of the church prove that for all of these different elements to come together – the necessary structure, order, administration, leadership, weekly meetings, and governances – the church herself must have the ability to flow with the movement of the Holy Spirit and the promise of continued spiritual activity within its members. The eleven functions of the church are:

- Preacher
- Missionary
- Dreamer and Visionary
- Interpreter of Dreams and Visions
- Intercessor
- Watchman and Gatekeeper
- Handmaiden and Menservant
- Scribe
- Spiritual Father and Mother
- Church Mother
- Mystic

WHY DO WE HAVE FUNCTIONS?

In order to understand why God has given us the functions, we must understand the order of the church and understand the different spiritual gifts that are given to the church.

The first form of "spiritual gifts" given to the church are in the form of leadership gifts, commonly called the five-fold ministry. The five-fold ministry consists of the offices of apostle, prophet, evangelist, pastor, and teacher. Ephesians 4 is clear about why these gifts exist:

- To equip God's people for works of service
- Build up the Body of Christ
- Reach unity in the faith and in the knowledge of the Son of God
- Become mature
- Attain the whole measure of the fullness of Christ
- Grow the church up so it is no longer consisting of infants
- Prevent the "tossing back and forth by the waves" which comes by changing teaching and cunning and deceptive doctrine
- Speak the truth in love
- Grow and build in love
- Each part of the Body doing its work

The reason leadership gifts are given to accomplish this task is simple: the church needs structure and order to bring the church to a place of maturity. Whether we like to deal with it or not, church history is full of denominations that have tried to alter God's established course for five-fold ministry leadership or, at some points, remove all forms of leadership, period. We all know the current state of Christianity across the board is not good, with traditional churches often suffering the most in terms of loss of members and attendance. As society changes and more and more social issues emerge, the improper leadership structure existing in these churches is unable to sustain itself and, as a result, leadership that does not conform to God's structure eventually falls, even if it takes awhile.

The thing that people tend to get confused about are exactly what each office of the five-fold is supposed to do and how these offices are to exist today. There are many people who believe in the five-fold ministry in theory, but are not applying the offices correctly in their own ministry. Some of these teachings include:

- People titling themselves with multiple offices (such as Apostle-Pastor or Apostle-Prophet)
- Believing that bishops outrank apostles and are superior in office to apostles

- Confusion over the pastor and what the pastor is supposed to do
- A decrease in the work and office of the teacher
- Believing everyone is called to the office of the evangelist (everyone is called to evangelize, not to be an evangelist; they are different)
- Assigning every coincidental observation to prophecy
- Denial of seminary and other higher-educational training for offices and ordained ministers

This list barely scratches the surface as to many of the problems we see in church today that all relate to misunderstandings of the five-fold ministry. The simplest way to resolve these questions is to examine what each office of the five-fold ministry is, and see how they work together, rather than in competition, within their respective offices.

To me, I don't see the five-fold ministry as a power struggle. I see five different offices, each one with something essential and different to do. It's not about anyone trying to be the head of the church (because that title belongs to Christ, and Christ alone), but each office serving its God-given purpose and monitoring the church through accountability and by serving in the specific and unique way that God has gifted each duly called leader in the church. (To gain a fuller understanding of the offices and the work of ministry, please get a copy of my book, *Awakening Christian Ministry: The Call To Serve Others As We Serve Jesus Christ*, if you have not already done so.)

- **Apostle** – Means "sent one" or "one who is sent." Apostles work to bring administrative structure and order to the church. Their primary call is to be sent to their respective assignments and to help establish and start churches as well as help those which already exist to continue to thrive and function efficiently (1 Corinthians 4:17, 1 Corinthians 12:28, Ephesians 2:20, Philippians 2:22). Apostles do this by working with leaders and helping to train, establish, and equip leaders to do their work effectively and with spiritual power. Apostles reveal the mysteries of God in their teaching (1 Corinthians 4:1-2) having received the revelation of God and having the ability to instruct, teach, and preach to nations (1 Timothy 2:1-7).

- **Prophet** – Means "one who speaks for God." Prophets speak the word of God to individuals, nations, the church, and even at times, the powers that be (Revelation 10:9-11). Prophets have the gift of bringing forth prophetic word, prophetic interpretation, and understanding to prophetic events. More than being about a prophet's line predicting houses and cars or trying to plug world headlines into prophecy, the work of the prophet is about understanding the words of God in our lives and about understanding how we fit into prophecy (Joel 2:28-31, 1 Corinthians 14:36-40). Through the prophet, we are able to receive God's word and understand its application for ourselves.

- **Evangelist** – Means "Christ bearer." The work of the evangelist is to reach the lost, the hurting, and those who do not know the Lord with the Gospel (Isaiah 61:1-3). The evangelist does not just go from church to church preaching, but works primarily with those who are what are commonly called "unsaved" or "non-believers."

- **Pastor** – Means "shepherd." The pastor is spoken of as being a shepherd because it is his or her job to care for the people who have been assigned to that spiritual "flock" as a part of that assembly (Jeremiah 3:15-16). The work of the shepherd is to care for the laity, or individuals who are not called to ministry (at least at that point in time under that leader) and to keep the church together through solid teaching, instruction, preaching, and helping to meet the practical needs of the congregation (Jeremiah 17:13-27).

- **Teacher** – Means "a teacher." It's pretty self-evident in definition to say a teacher…well…teaches, but teaching has become a lost art in many Christian churches. With an over-emphasis on offices perceived to be "higher" than others in the five-fold (apostles, prophets), teaching fades in the light of entertaining preaching and a lack of proper structure. Teachers teach about the Scriptures, about essential things of the faith, they may write books or curricula, they may teach Sunday School or adult education, they may work in Christian schools or Seminaries, and they do so as they make the essential things of God practical and understandable to the church across the board (Romans 12:4-8, James 3:2-12).

In compliment to the five-fold ministry, we also have the different positions of bishop, elder, and deacon. These three positions are called "appointments" because they are jobs that apostles appoint within the church in order to assist the five-fold ministry. Bishops, elders, and deacons are not offices that are a part of the five-fold ministry, but rather, the overseeing aspects of the helps ministries in each church and within the church as a whole. The appointments indicate an individual desires to do the work and is appointed to do it; it is not a life-long calling or something that God deposits within an individual to do in the same sense of fulfilling a calling (1 Timothy 3:1). While sometimes five-fold ministry leaders may have what's called a "dual ordination" to an appointment and an office, the work of the appointments is different than the work of the five-fold. Bishops and elders are not interchangeable titles for pastors, and deacons are not over pastors in authority. The work of the appointments, while just as important, are different from the work and function of the five-fold ministry. Understanding this helps us understand in a deeper sense why we need to have these different categories of gifts, works, and callings, and why all of these things are different, yet just as important, in order to keep the church functioning properly. (To gain a fuller understanding of the offices, appointments, and the work of ministry, please get a copy of my books, *Awakening Christian Ministry: The Call To Serve Others As We Serve Jesus Christ* and *Ministry School Boot Camp: Training For Helps Ministries,*

Appointments and Beyond, if you have not already done so.)

- **Bishop** – Means "an overseer." The work of the bishop is to do just that – oversee something. This means that the proper context of a bishop is an individual who is assigned to keep track of a work and maintain its functioning either within a church, a church para-organization, or in connection with overseeing an area for ministry maintenance by an apostle. Bishops ensure proper teaching comes forth in every ministry and that things are maintained according to directives (1 Timothy 3:1-7, Titus 1:6-16). They serve as a means of proper communication and implementation of structure. Nowhere in the Bible are bishops ever considered, nor regarded, on the same level as nor superior to that of the office of the apostle.

- **Elder** – Means "an older or mature person." The description of the "elders" as "older" is often used in the Bible to indicate someone who is physically older in age, but that assignment is to identify the maturity of an individual. It also indicates one in a superior ministry, or of a higher office than another. In the context of the elders of the church, they are appointed by apostles to assist the pastor of a church in the needs of that congregation: teaching, preaching, and seeing to it that the people of the congregation receive the fullness of doctrine and education in their work (1 Peter 5:1-10, James 5:14-15). Elders do not work beyond a local congregation.

- **Deacon** – Means "attendant" or "servant." The work of the deacon is to serve in a literal sense, extending proper stewardship and assistance to the five-fold ministry and to the congregation (1 Timothy 3:8-13). Assigned by apostles to assist the local congregations as needed, deacons do their work through practical needs ministry: making sure the disenfranchised are cared for, operating social Gospel ministry work, and assisting leaders (Acts 6:1-15).

Then we have the area of charismatic spiritual gifts. Earlier we talked about the *didomi*, or leadership gifts (the five-fold ministry). Charismatic spiritual gifts are different from the five-fold ministry and appointments because they are open to everybody in the body of Christ, not just those who are gifted in areas of leadership. I Corinthians 12 explains to us why we have charismatic gifts:

- To proclaim Jesus as Lord
- To walk in the power of the Holy Spirit
- To operate different kinds of gifts
- To operate different kinds of service
- To operate different kinds of working
- To understand the Holy Spirit at work through these different kinds of gifts, and realize the work of God is active through all of these different ministries
- For the common good
- To express the diversity present in the Body, and the oneness of all of us who are in Christ

The charismatic gifts are found in I Corinthians 12 and in Romans 12 (To gain a fuller understanding of the offices, appointments, and the work of ministry, please get a copy of my book, *Ministry School Boot Camp: Training For Helps Ministries, Appointments and Beyond*, if you have not already done so). They are:

- **Word of wisdom** – The ability to give insight, relevance, and revelation into a situation that you know nothing about or are not directly a part of. It is a form of prophecy, but it differs in that it often requires the action of the receiver of the revelation. In other words: if someone does not act upon the wise word given to them, they will most likely continue to deal with their pressing or difficult situation.

- **Word of knowledge** – The ability to give applicable knowledge about a situation that you know nothing about or are not directly a part of. Like the word of wisdom, it is also a form of prophecy but varies because it may not require obedience or action on the part of a receiver. A word of knowledge directly imparts something about or into a situation, rather than requiring direct action on the part of the recipient.

- **Faith** – We learn in Hebrews 11:1 that *Faith is the substance of things hoped for, the evidence of things not seen.* This means that faith is the substance (or stuff) of something hoped for, the evidence (or proof) of things not seen. Faith is a spiritual gift that it is clear there are different levels of and different proportions given to each believer. To have the gift of faith is to endure, trusting and focusing on God above all other things in life.

- **Healing** – We know that healing is the spiritual ability to make a sick individual well, but it is tempting to think that healing is all about physical healing. Yes, physical healing from an illness, malady, or physical issue is a part of healing and does exist. There are many other ways, however, that people receive healing. A gift of healing can also be manifested through emotional, mental, or spiritual healing that is needed in an individual. Most often this is done via laying on of hands and/or prayer, but healing can also come about through counseling, praying with someone through a situation, offering comfort, or being there for a person.

- **Miracles** – A miracle is a supernatural occurrence that has no explanation in the natural or scientific realm. It is a working of God, rather than one of magic, chance, or cause and effect. To work miracles means that someone is able to do the impossible by the power of God without any other way to explain or define it.

- **Prophecy** – Prophecy is a loaded topic because it is frequently misunderstood and those who operate a gift of prophecy are often automatically assumed to be a prophet.

With prophecy as a charismatic gift, God can give anyone a prophetic word or revelation without that person being a full-time prophet, devoted to speaking the word of God consistently. The gift of prophecy flows within an individual at God's movement, as it is needed. True prophecy manifests as an individual sees or foretells an event, has a dream or encounter with God that reveals something, operates in prophetic interpretation, or works in the arts (writing, dance, music, etc.).

- **Discernment of spirits** – The ability to tell if a spirit or a motive is good or bad, right or wrong, of God or not of God. It is the gift of "sorting things out" in the spiritual realm.

- **Diverse tongues** – Also called the "baptism of the Holy Spirit," we often call it "speaking in tongues." When someone has this gift, an individual speaks in their prayer language of heaven rather than in an earthly language.

- **Interpretation of tongues** – If a word is given to the believers in tongues, it must be interpreted so it can be understood. Interpretation can mean that tongues are heard directly by someone in their own language (as happened at Pentecost) or that an individual interprets them by the Holy Spirit for a congregation.

- **Ministry service** – Any gift offered to be of help for the work of ministry is considered "ministry service."

- **Teaching** – Like the charismatic gift of prophecy, teaching can also be a gift that is exercised without someone operating in the office of teacher. A gift of teaching indicates someone is able to teach from time to time or on occasion without teaching full-time or as a predominate calling. This can manifest through a class, a Sunday or weekly instruction, writing, media ministry, or any other way that teaching may be accomplished.

- **Exhortation** – Exhortation is a big, long word that means to "edify" or "build up." Someone who exhorts is someone who builds up and edifies someone's Christian walk in their relationship with God. It means to do more than just encourage, because in exhortation, something is being edified with strength and empowerment.

- **Leading** – Someone who is a leader, but is not in the five-fold ministry, would be said to have a gift of leadership or "leading." This can apply to an individual who assists in a team effort or work, or oversees a committee, or somehow facilitates teamwork and group activities in order to get something accomplished.

- **Giving (mercy)** – In giving (or in being merciful), an individual has the ability to reflect the heart of God and extend a sense of love and mercy to another when someone is in need of such.

In a certain sense, there may be many different ways in which spiritual gifts overlap in our lives. We may operate in many of them at different points as needed (maybe a few times in our lifetimes) and we may have some that are stronger and we exercise on a regular basis. Some people think it's important to emphasize using the gifts we feel we are "good at" or "better suit" us, while others think it is a better idea to teach on all the gifts and then give them opportunities to walk in all of them. I think that the appropriate response to spiritual gifts lies somewhere in the middle. The reason spiritual gifts are spoken of as being spiritual gifts is because they are given by God, as needed, as He wills, and that means leadership and those trained in understanding these different things need to be attentive to the movements of individuals as pertain to spiritual gifts and their unique operations. Yes, everyone in the church needs to know and understand what spiritual gifts are and ways to recognize their operation. Yes, we all need to know how the Spirit moves through the gifts and ways that the gifts complement each other. At the same time, if someone does not have a spiritual gift, no amount of pushing, training, or prodding is going to make that gift appear. Rather than insisting that people learn how to operate in all the gifts, we should discern what people are able to do and help them better understand those gifts, monitoring their activity as leaders of the church.

All of the things I have mentioned so far are vital and essential to church function. We need leadership, we need people who are in helps to assist leaders, and we need spiritual gifts in order to keep the flow and function of the church active and relevant. Many stop here when it comes to church structure and order, and that means an awful lot of things are left out of church. What about nursery? What about a dream someone needs interpreted? What about people who see visions? What about cleaning the church? If we go by the list of things we have already discussed, one could say that these other aspects should be handled by the groups of people already mentioned. The problem with this line of thinking is that the Bible does list other things and other practical duties by name that do not fit in with any of these abovementioned categories. That must mean they relate to something else, in a different way, than to what has already been discussed.

We have functions because there are things that are not simply covered by other areas of church operation and do not require a formal office, appointment, or gifting in order to perform them. These things are, in a general heading, called the works of the church.

THE WORKS OF THE CHURCH

The "works of the church" is a general heading I have assigned to church work that is for everyone in the church to participate in, from the top on down. They are run as ministries by lay volunteers and organized in a setting for church work and overseen by the appointment ministries (bishop, elder, deacon). They are works that help keep the church going by performing essential and valuable services for the church, such as:

- Announcements
- Office/business work
- Ushers/greeters
- Altar work
- Praise and worship team/choir
- Audio/visual ministry
- Arts/dance ministry
- Children's ministry
- Youth ministry
- Women's/Men's ministry
- Building maintenance
- Hospitality
- Social outreach
- Street evangelism

None of these works require a calling or an appointment, and while they are a great source for us to operate in our different spiritual gifts, they do not all require spiritual gifts to get the job done. This list also contains thing that simply need doing and that someone needs to rise to the task to make sure things get done. Rather than being seen as a disgrace or something of "lesser" importance, the maturity required to do the things that need doing without complaint and without argument are essential to church operation.

Within this general heading of works or the helps of the church, we have the heading of the functions of the church. I have designated the functions as a part of the works because they are indeed a work of the church, one does not need to be ordained nor appointed in order to serve in a function, and they help the church to meet the needs of all the different people encountered through the different helps ministries and general laity of the church. Being found in both the Old and New Testament, functions have helped and assisted God's people throughout time, and are neither an old thing nor a new thing, but a now thing. Those in functions may also help those in leadership in an interpersonal way (even as found in other leaders themselves), by interpreting a dream, sharing a vision, or assisting in the growth of the church by performing works unique to the functional purposes.

HOW MANY FUNCTIONS CAN ONE PERSON HAVE?

Because functions are something that arise as needed, many individuals in church will have many experiences with different functions in their lifetimes. It is possible to operate more than one function at once, and it is also possible to operate in a function as needed for a period of time, and then never operate it again or only operate in it from time to time.

HOW FUNCTIONS WORK

The functions arise as they are needed and depend on an individual's spiritual perceptiveness and insights into the spiritual realm. In a deeper sense, the functions operate as an individual is able to understand and observe needs in the world around them, and see how those needs can be met spiritually. For example: interpreting a dream for someone as guided by God-given insights into that dream is an obvious way of observing and meeting spiritual needs, but preaching accomplishes the same thing through the means of proclaiming the Word of God and matching a message to a group of people. This means that the individuals who operate in functions must have relatively good spiritual training, proper insight and understanding into spiritual gifts and the ways in which they move through a person, and their own position in the Body of Christ. Functions enhance spiritual gifts, callings, appointments and works as they help the church to operate beyond ritual, rite, and doctrine.

In the next chapters, we will examine the eleven different functions and at the end, a special chapter on when offices serve as functions for five-fold ministry leaders. Gaining clarity on the functions will help explain many aspects of church work and ministry that are frequently overlooked, and bless us as we see

God's magnificent church design manifest in each one of us doing our work.

Two ● Preacher

Well some say John was a Baptist,
Some say John was a Jew,
But I say John was a preacher
And my Bible says so, too.
— Topsy Chapman, "Roll, Jordan Roll"[1]

PREACHING is one of the most desired aspects of church life and church purpose. We push people into the pulpit like it's nobody's business, thinking that someone has truly achieved something if they are preaching and in a preaching work. Many think it is the most desirable thing in the world to be a preacher, and many more assume that being able to preach means one has a calling to ministry. Even though this may be true, it is perfectly possible someone may preach and not have a calling to ministry, because the Bible does speak of both options as a possibility.

Preaching is different from teaching (which is spoken of as a spiritual gift) and has its own unique purpose. It is spoken of as a command, as a discipline, and as something that has been done, believe it or not, all throughout Biblical history. Even though we may view preaching in a certain way and with a certain traditional style, the world of preaching is important for the sake of functionality and continuation of the church, as those who have never heard are stirred to acceptance and those who have heard are re-ignited by the hearing of the Word.

TEXT STUDY

Mark 16:15-20

POWER TEXTS

Ezra 6:13-15, Jonah 1:2-3, Matthew 3:1-12, Matthew 4:12-17, Matthew 23:1-12, Acts 8:4-8, Acts 16:6-10, Romans 10:5-18, 1 Corinthians 1:13-25, 1 Corinthians 9:13-18, 2 Timothy 4:1-5.

POWER VERSE

Mark 16:15:

- *"And He said unto them, Go ye into all the world, and preach the Gospel to every creature."*

- *"And then He told them, 'You are to go into all the world and preach the Good News to everyone, everywhere.'"* (TLB)

- *"He said to them, 'Go into all the world and preach the Gospel to every creature.'"* (NET)

- *"Then He said to them, 'You must go out to the whole world and proclaim the Gospel to every creature.'"* (PHILLIPS)

- *"And He said to them, Go into all the world and preach and publish openly the good news (the Gospel) to every creature [of the whole human race]."* (AMP)

- *"And He said to them, 'Go into all the world and preach the Gospel to the whole creation.'"* (RSV)

POWER WORDS

- **Go** – From the Greek word *poreuomai* which means, "to lead over, carry over, transfer."[2]

- **All** – From the Greek word *hapas* which means "quite, all, the whole, all together, all."[3]

- **World** – From the Greek word *kosmos* which means, "an apt and harmonious arrangement or constitution, order, government; ornament, decoration, adornment, i.e. the arrangement of the stars, 'the heavenly hosts', as the ornament of the heavens. I Pet. 3:3; the world, the universe; the circle of the earth, the earth; the inhabitants of the earth, men, the human race; the ungodly multitude; the whole mass of men alienated from God, and therefore hostile to the cause of Christ; world affairs, the aggregate of things earthly; any aggregate or general collection of particulars of any sort."[4]

- **Preach** – From the Greek word *kerusso*, which means, "to be a herald, to officiate as a herald; to proclaim after the manner of a herald; to publish, proclaim openly: something which has been done; used of the public proclamation of the gospel and matters pertaining to it, made by John the Baptist, by Jesus, by the apostles and other Christian teachers."[5]

- **Gospel** – From the Greek word *euaggelion* which means, "a reward for good tidings; good tidings, the glad tidings of the kingdom of God soon to be set up, and subsequently also of Jesus the Messiah, the founder of this kingdom. After the death of Christ, the term comprises also the preaching of (concerning) Jesus Christ as having suffered death on the cross to procure eternal salvation for the men in the kingdom of God, but as restored to life and exalted to the right hand of God in heaven, thence to return in majesty to consummate the kingdom of God, the glad tidings of salvation through Christ, the proclamation of the grace of God manifest and pledged in Christ, the gospel, as the messianic rank of Jesus was proved by his words, his deeds, and his death, the narrative of the sayings, deeds, and death of Jesus Christ came to be called the gospel or glad tidings."[6]

- **Every** – From the Greek word *pas* which means "individually; each, every, any, all, the whole, everyone, all things, everything; collectively, some of all types."[7]

- **Creature** – From the Greek word *ktisis* which means, "the act of founding, establishing, building etc., the act of creating, creation, creation i.e. thing created, institution, ordinance."[8]

HISTORICAL CONTEXT

In ancient settings, important information was circulated by word of mouth. Without computers, telephones, internet access, and easily written documents, news travelled fast as it was proclaimed and spoken from one person to another. Preaching, or heralding news openly, was one of the most common ways to convey an essential and important message. When Jesus commanded His first followers to go and preach the Gospel, He was telling them to go and circulate information about Him as they heralded the news that He was the living Son of God, alive forevermore.

NOTES ON TEXT

Being told to preach to every creature on earth sounds intimidating, but it gives the Gospel a unique method of transmission because it focuses on individual impact. It was God's desire that the Gospel personally impact every life, around the world, in an undeniable and unavoidable way. Giving the assignment to preach ensured that people would transmit the message with their words and their lives and that every person who is a part of the order of creation would have the opportunity to change their lives by believing in this essential message.

POWER POINTS

- Preaching is distinguished from teaching by virtue of the nature and style of the message. The Bible clarifies that teaching is dedicated to instruction, while preaching makes a message known and opens it up to others in a way that commands their attention. Many times signs and wonders confirms the message, because these help keep people's attention and verify the message at hand (Mark 16:15-20, Acts 8:4-8). The reason the Gospel was to be preached to all of creation is because it gives people the opportunity to be saved from eternal alienation from God. We understand the command to preach the Gospel to all creation as a command for all believers, both those who are in ordained ministry and those who are not (Ezra 6:14). It is also not just a work restricted for that of the evangelist, but one that we are all commanded to do, prepared for things both in season and out of season (2 Timothy 4:1-5). This allows for the work of the preacher to be open to all, along with the signs that are to follow those who believe: casting out demons, speaking in new tongues, overcoming the power of the enemy (taking up serpents), protection from harm (not being harmed by poison) and laying hands on the sick, and seeing the sick get well (Mark 16:15-20).

- The work of preaching is not unique to the New Testament, although in the New Testament, it was to be something done to all of creation, rather than just a specific or assigned group of people. Under the direction of right preaching, ministries are built and work prospers (Ezra 6:13-15).

- Preachers are sent to proclaim word, and should be supported by those to whom they preach (1 Corinthians 1:13-25, 1 Corinthians 9:13-18). The preacher, given a message and a command to preach, must be careful not to ignore that duty and must be diligent about speaking the word, no matter what it is or where one has to go in order to convey God's word (Acts 16:6-10). As we can see in the example of the Prophet Jonah, preachers are given a specific message to relay to individuals. We know in the New Covenant, we are given the word of the Gospel (Mark 16:15-20). Once God gives the preacher the word, they must be obedient unto it for face God for their disobedience. The Prophet Jonah is a great example of what happens when a preacher disobeys God's command to preach (Jonah 1:2-3).

- A common theme throughout the Scriptures for preaching is the message of repentance, which is one that centers around reception and proclamation of the Gospel. To "repent" literally means to turn around, to change one's mind, and to go in a new or different direction. As the work of John the Baptist reflects, the word that the Kingdom of heaven was so near you could reach out and touch it came with a word of repentance and a baptism for remission of sins. (Matthew 3:1-12). This tells us that true preaching prepares the heart to receive Christ, just as John's work prepared individuals to do the same. After John completed his work, Jesus too stepped up and began preaching about the Kingdom of heaven that was at hand (Matthew 4:12-17).

- Jesus Himself warns us against the dangers of not "practicing what we preach." This means the preacher must be very careful to abide and live by the very things they teach and proclaim. Rather than preaching in order to be seen of individuals and make other people think we are grand, we should be preaching as servants of Christ and of mankind, not seeking to exalt ourselves above anyone else (Matthew 23:1-12).

- The Bible itself teaches that the Word of God spreads by preaching, not by reading the Scriptures. While there is nothing wrong with reading the Scriptures, the faith that must come forth that proclaims Jesus is Lord comes by hearing the preached word, the revelation for those people in that time. It is a clear example of order, as the one who preaches is sent, the one who hears the preached word, and those who hear have the opportunity to believe in Christ and be saved in His Name. The feet that carry those who preach are beautiful, because they bring good news (Romans 10:5-18).

Ways we can encourage and support preachers

There are many ways that we can support the work of the Gospel through those that preach. Even if individuals do not preach as a part of their ministries, every preacher needs the encouragement of the saints in order to help them proclaim the Gospel to every creature, in accordance with Jesus' command.

- **Support ministers** – Even though not all preachers are always five-fold ministry ministers or may not all work in ministry as a full-time job, the work of ministry needs to be supported through tithes, offerings, volunteering to assist when needed, and stepping up to support the work of those who do persist in Gospel proclamation, year in and year out.

- **Support young preachers with encouragement** – When a person is a "young preacher," that means they are new to preaching (they have preached less than five sermons or have been preaching less than two years, whichever comes first). Being a new preacher is a difficult thing, because it seems like you have too many opportunities to mess up and not enough to succeed. Young preachers also try to mimic someone else's style, so coming into their own over time requires a lot of support and encouragement. As a young preacher develops, be there to encourage and support them.

- **Embrace different styles of preaching** – When I looked up the word "preaching" to find a definition, I came across many different words and terms for "preaching," including "sermon," "homily," and "speech." In my understanding of preaching, I never thought about those words being interchangeable with preaching, but it turns out that, in terms of tradition, they are. There are many different styles to preaching that adapt and change between cultures, nations, and individual ways a person may be directed by God to give a message. Not all preaching has to be formal, traditional, or within the confines of current American entertainment. Listen to some different preachers to hear ways that the Word is spoken all throughout the world.

PREACHERS IN HISTORY

There are many known preachers and some preachers who were not as well-known. Take a look at four individuals you may or may not have heard of – and the work they did as preachers for the Lord.

- **George Whitefield (1714-1770)** – Unless you are devout student of all things church history, George Whitefield probably isn't someone you have heard of. George Whitefield was an Anglican clergyman who helped to spread the Great Awakening in Britain and the United States. He has long been considered one of the founders of Methodism and is also one of the roots of the Evangelical movement. It was his preaching during revival meetings that started what we now call the "Great Awakening," a mass movement of intense religious fervor and conversion in the 1700s.[9]

- **Zilpha Elaw (1790-?)** – Zilpha Elaw was born as a free woman and raised in Philadelphia by a deeply religious family. She lived with a Quaker family after the death of her mother and, upon seeing a vision of Jesus, she became a part of a Methodist society in 1808. Later in 1817, Zilpha attended a revival which put her in a visionary state, after which she preached for the first time. Throughout her life, Zilpha Elaw experienced visitations and visions, and despite trying to start a school, she became an itinerant preacher for over thirteen years in the United States and then preached for five years and over one thousand sermons in Great Britain.[10]

- **Rachel Artemissa Harper Sizelove (1864-1941)** – We don't have a lot of details about Rachel Sizelove's life, but we do know that she was a woman touched directly by the Azusa Street Revival in 1906. She took her message all the way back home to Springfield, Missouri and then started holding small home meetings (called "cottage meetings"). One who experienced a particular prophetic vision of the impact of Pentecostalism on the world, Rachel Sizelove preached to many audiences in her lifetime, impacting many with the Gospel.[11]

- **Martin Luther King, Jr. (1929-1968)** – Most people know about Martin Luther King, Jr. and his extensive work in the Civil Rights Movement. Advocating non-violent civil disobedience, Martin Luther King, Jr. was a part of and organized several marches that were influential in desegregation and many legal changes that were unjust toward African-Americans. Many do not know that Martin Luther King, Jr. was also a Baptist preacher and ordained minister. We cannot escape the reality that being a preacher profoundly influenced his views and his work, and that one of the most notable figures of the Civil Rights Movement was a preacher!

QUESTIONS AND ANSWERS

- **Why is preaching an essential point in the salvation process?**

As I spoke briefly on earlier, the Bible tells us that *Faith cometh by hearing, and hearing by the Word of God* (Romans 10:17). While I sincerely laud the work and efforts of those who have labored to make sure we have the Scriptures available in printed form and in our common language, the Scriptures themselves nowhere state that faith comes by reading the Scriptures. The main reason for this is because expecting people to be able to read the Scriptures and interpret them perfectly, each man and woman for themselves, is elitist. For thousands of years, people were illiterate and had no access to the Scriptures because copies were not readily available. Does this mean that these people were not saved and had no chance for salvation? Of course not! Preaching the Word – speaking out God's good news of the Gospel and telling people about Christ – is the only way that the Gospel can go forth into all the world and impact every life. No matter where someone is, what someone's level of education is, no matter what they do, or who they are, everyone can be reached by the preaching of the Gospel. This gives the Gospel a unique touch, a personal touch, and one that can impact as many lives as possible. It does mean that it takes longer than through another method, and that this work will be done until the time when Jesus returns.

- **Do preachers have to be licensed and ordained?**

Technically the things that require a minister to be licensed and ordained are things done by that minister that have legal standing. For example, baptisms, funerals, weddings, communion services, and ordinations are all ceremonies that do not just carry with them spiritual significance, but legal relevance, as well. Most minister's licenses, however, also list preaching along with the legal ceremonies. Why is this?

Technically, preaching is not a legal entity, and most churches allow individuals within their membership to preach without a license. If someone is a part of a church and they are asked to preach a message, they are able to do so without paperwork. In some states, a license is not required to preach anywhere. There are some states, however, that require a license to preach if you are considered a visiting minister or an itinerant preacher. For this reason, if an individual plans on being a preacher beyond their own covering ministry's immediate church borders, they do need to have a minister's license. If a minister is in training or in house, no such paperwork is required.

Ordination is required for the five-fold ministry offices, and not just for preaching. If someone is called to an office of the five-fold ministry and they also preach, they need both ordination and licensure.

- **Can preachers be married?**

Nothing in the Bible says they can't. We see examples of preachers who were married, and preachers who were single. We also see many that we don't know if they were married or not, either way, which tells us it is not a point of consequence to be married or single and be a preacher.

- **Can women preach?**

Some might argue the point, but yes, women can be preachers. The proclamation to preach the Gospel to all nations is for all believers, not specifically for men. The functions are not, as a rule, regulated to one sex or the other. In the instances of sex-specific functions, there is always an equivalent function for the opposite sex.

- **Should preachers wear robes or clerical wear?**

Minister's robes are used for certain rites, rituals, and ordinances, which do not necessarily relate to the work of preaching (and there are many ministers who refrain from wearing robes for any number of reasons). This means if someone is functioning in the work of a preacher and is not ordained to ministry (which is more or less what we are looking at), they are not performing rites, rituals, and ordinances for people. The work of a preacher is a functional one, and that means attire should match the purpose of preaching work, whether done in the street, in a church, in a foreign country, or in an event. If an event requires a robe, then the preacher should align with the requirements, but the robe must be plain and basic, and not in any way confused with the robe of an ordained minister.

- **Should preachers receive training?**

Preachers should be trained in accordance with their covering ministry, especially if they are receiving a license in order to preach. Preacher's training does not have to be as comprehensive as minister's training, but should relate to information and things that will help that preacher excel in the pulpit. Preachers should be educated in different styles of preaching, in Scripture studies and exegesis, in Bible history and culture, and in church history, among any other area of education that a church can think of that will help a preacher proclaim the Gospel in a powerful and effective way.

DISCUSSION, STUDY AND REVIEW QUESTIONS

1. How was information circulated in ancient times? When Jesus commanded His followers to go and preach the Gospel, what was He in effect telling them to do?

2. How does preaching give the Gospel a unique means of transmission for the message? What did giving the assignment to preach do?

3. How is preaching distinguished from teaching? Why do signs and wonders often accompany an important message? Why was the Gospel to be preached in all of creation? Who is the command to preach the Gospel for? What signs are to follow those who believe?

4. Is the work of preaching unique to the New Testament? How does it vary in the New Testament from the Old Testament? What happens when people follow right preaching?

5. How are preachers instructed as to how they deliver a word? How should they be supported? What happens to preachers when they disobey God? Who is an example of this? What happened to him?

6. What is a common theme for preaching in the Scriptures? Why is this message important? What does the word "repent" mean? What does true preaching prepare the heart to do? How was John the Baptist's preaching connected to Jesus' preaching?

7. Why does Jesus warn us about "practicing what we preach?" What does this mean? Why should someone preach?

8. How does the Bible say the Word of God spreads? What is the clear order as pertains to hearing and receiving faith?

9. What are some ways we can encourage preachers?

10. Who were some notable preachers in history?

11. Discuss and share some of the questions and answers found in the "Questions and Answers" section. What did you learn that you did not know about preachers and preaching? What did you learn that changed your mind about an opinion you might have had prior about preachers and preaching? How did learning about specific issues related to preachers help you to grow in your understanding of preaching? The church? Your own relationship with God?

12. Who is your favorite preacher? Why are they your favorite?

Three ● MISSIONARY

We talk of the Second Coming; half the world has never heard of the first.
— Oswald J. Smith[1]

FOR centuries, missionaries went forth with the Gospel to start churches, educate individuals, and proclaim God's Word in foreign lands. None of these were short-term projects, but ones that required the individuals to make a long-term investment in their spiritual work. They had to move to a foreign land, learn the culture, learn the language, sometimes translate the Bible into other languages, and devote their entire selves to the work of the Gospel in a strange place. Missionaries fought for their lives (and sometimes lost their lives in the process), pioneered the Gospel in new lands, and tirelessly persevered so those who had never heard of Jesus Christ could know that Jesus was with them and that God loved them.

The term "missionary" is not ever found in the Bible, although the foundations for missionary work are found in the Bible and the commands that missionaries live through their work are Biblical. At one point in history, missions were not only common, they were considered the highest form of service to God. With changes in society and in church over the past one hundred years, it is rare to see individuals who are willing to make the commitment to long-term mission work.

This does not mean that missions are dead, however. It does mean that we should support true missionaries and that we should learn more about this work, especially as the number of missions has dropped over the years. It is vital that we, as church members, respect and honor missionaries: past, present, and future.

TEXT STUDY

2 Kings 17:24-41

POWER TEXTS

Psalm 96:1-10, Psalm 107:23-32, Isaiah 6:1-13, Isaiah 56:1-8, Jonah 3:1-10, Matthew 24:9-14, Matthew 28:16-20, Acts 1:6-8, Acts 13:46-52, Ephesians 2:11-22, Revelation 14:6-7,14-16.

POWER VERSE

2 Kings 17:27-28:

- *"Then the king of Assyria commanded, saying, Carry thither one of the priests whom ye brought from thence; and let them go and dwell there, and let him teach them the manner of the God of the land. Then one of the priests whom they had carried away from Samaria came and dwelt in Bethel, and taught them how they should fear the LORD."*

- *"Then the king of Assyria gave this order: 'Have one of the priests you took captive from Samaria go back to live there and teach the people what the god of the land requires.' So one of the priests who had been exiled from Samaria came to live in Bethel and taught them how to worship the LORD."* (NIV)

- *"So Assyria's king commanded, 'Return one of the priests that you exiled from there. He should go back and live there. He should teach them the religious practices of the local god.' So one of the priests who had been exiled from Samaria went back. He lived in Bethel and taught the people how to worship the LORD."* (CEB)

- *"And the king of Asshur commandeth, saying, 'Cause to go thither one of the priests whom ye removed thence, and they go and dwell there, and he doth teach them the custom of the God of the land.' And one of the priests whom they removed from Samaria cometh in, and dwelleth in Beth-El, and he is teaching them ow they do fear Jehovah."* (YLT)

- *"The king of Assyria then commanded, 'Send one of the exiled priests back to Samaria. Let him live there and teach the new residents the religious customs of the God of the land.' So one of the priests who had been exiled from Samaria returned to Bethel and taught the new residents how to worship the LORD."* (NLT)

- *"Then the king of Assyria commanded, Take to Samaria one of the priests you brought from there, and let him [and his helpers] go and live there and let him teach the people the law of the God of the land. So one of the priests whom they had carried away from Samaria came and dwelt in Bethel and taught them how they should fear and revere the Lord."* (AMP)

POWER WORDS

- **Carry** – From the Hebrew word *yalak* which means, "to go, walk, come."[2]

- **Priests** – From the Hebrew word *kohen* which means "priest, principal officer or chief ruler."[3]

- **Dwell** – From the Hebrew word *yashab* which means, "to dwell, remain, sit, abide."[4]

- **Teach** – From the Hebrew word *yarah* which means, "to throw, shoot, cast, pour."[5]

- **Manner** – From the Hebrew word *mishpat* which means, "judgment, justice, ordinance."[6]

- **Fear** – From the Hebrew word *yare'* which means "individually; each, every, any, all, the whole, everyone, all things, everything; collectively, some of all types."[7]

- **LORD** – From the Hebrew word *Yehovah* which means, "Jehovah = "the existing One;" the proper name of the one true God."[8]

HISTORICAL CONTEXT

When cities (and nations) were overthrown or taken by force by a new government, the first question these governmental powers dealt with was what to do with the remaining captives. Oftentimes captives were treated as slaves or were somehow considered secondary citizens, unable to exercise the same rights as existing citizens. The Assyrian government, being a part of the world of polytheism, had no hesitation in worshipping Jehovah, the true God of the Hebrews, along with their other gods. In order to learn the culture of the Hebrews, the Assyrians set up priests to help with this process.

NOTES ON TEXT

Even though the priests were invited in by the pagan leaders who had their own agenda about what was to come as a result of the priests' work, the Hebrew priests were sent on a mission: one where they were to teach and train the people in the ways of God and in the ways of the service of God. They were in an entirely foreign nation, surrounded by foreign gods, foreign teachings, and foreign customs, sent there to train the people in the ways of God. As the situation in 2 Kings 17 proves: missions are not always successful, but when given the opportunity to go on one, the ultimate work is always one that God is working behind the scenes.

POWER POINTS

- A missionary is an individual who, as moved by their faith or position in the Kingdom, goes to proclaim the Gospel in a foreign country or in a territory that is foreign to that individual. The term "missionary" indicates a person with a mission. More than just going to preach, missionaries go into unknown territories with long-term plans to teach the people there about God and to establish centers of worship. Like the priests in 2 Kings 17, missionaries go in to live and teach the people what God requires and how to worship God rightly and powerfully (2 Kings 17:24-28).

- An individual may be called on to go and serve in a missions setting by a higher-up in ministry or may be sent directly by God Himself. Not all mission work is successful, because establishing the worship of God in places where God is unknown or foreign is extremely difficult. Sometimes people attempt to take the worship of God and mix it with their existing cultural worship, or some reject it all together. Sometimes mission work is successful only among a few. That does not mean that missions are a failure, or that a missionary is a bad missionary. There are many ways to "plow the field," so to speak, and establish a nation in the worship of God. Sometimes it takes many generations, and this is why missions from age to age are so vitally important (2 Kings 17:29-41).

- Missionaries reveal the true universal nature of the church and the church's work (Matthew 28:16-20). Jesus did not tell us to stay among ourselves, but to go into all the world and make disciples. It is easy to think that church work begins and ends in our local congregations, but this is not the case. There are many who still have yet to hear the Gospel who are beyond our own local church communities. The work of the missionary: the heart of going forth with God's mission reminds us that the church is not just exclusive to one group, but is universal and accessible to each and every person who is willing to receive it. Even though many will turn away from the faith and times will grow hard, the Gospel is to be preached as a testimony to all nations before Jesus returns (Matthew 24:9-14).

- A missionary may desire their mission, or avoid their mission. We can see in the book of Jonah that while he might have been a prophet with a history of service, he did not desire his mission to Nineveh to preach repentance to that people. As a result of his mission, the people of Nineveh turned from their ways and turned toward what was right (Jonah 3:1-10). The Prophet Isaiah desired the mission to go forth, stepping up with the heart of "Here am I. Send me!" (Isaiah 6:1-13). Some missions are harder than others, and there are all different responses to the work of missions, as depend on the individual missionary.

- Missionaries operate on God's divine power that was promised to us in Acts 1: to go forth and be witnesses to the ends of the earth, because the harvest is ripe and ready (Acts 1:6-8, Revelation 14:6-7,14-16). They receive this divine power as they receive the word of God, first spoken to them, then spoken by them and lived by them. Missionaries are individuals who live their faith, who shine as light to the nations, that the end result may be salvation to the ends of the earth. The missionary recognizes being of service, especially in areas where social needs go unmet, is essential to being an effective witness of the Gospel (Acts 13:46-52).

- Many wonder why anyone would want to be a missionary. Missionaries see God work for them in ways that they would have never expected, nor imagined, as they go out into the deep for the Lord (Psalm 107:23-32). For this reason, the missionary has a special word not just for those they reach in missions, but for those who remain a part of local churches wherever they are. They have seen and encountered the salvation of God up close and personal, watching Him save and deliver, time and time again, and see that He truly is God, time and time again. The missionary reminds us that we are to ascribe to God all that is due Him, and that among all nations, our Lord reigns (Psalm 96:1-10).

- Recognizing that salvation is for all, the missionary reminds each and every one of us of the fact that God loves everyone and desires everyone to be saved. The missionary is a powerful type of that time to come when all nations will worship God in His holiness after Jesus returns, and that the door is open for people to worship along with us, becoming a part of His church right now, today (Isaiah 56:1-8). We praise God for all who become a part of the church through the work of missionaries who prove to all that Jesus is our peace, and that politics and social hostility must cease in His presence, because the missionaries themselves are willing to lay down their lives so all can become a part of the household of faith, living by His Spirit (Ephesians 2:11-22).

WAYS WE CAN ENCOURAGE AND SUPPORT MISSIONARIES

There are many ways that we can support the work of the Gospel through those that answer the Great Commission by serving as missionaries. The work of missions is important and essential, and it is vital that we find new ways to help missionaries as they go forth into distant places to do this essential work.

- **Be a part of missions** – Not everyone is supposed to travel to foreign territories or countries to proclaim and live the Gospel. It's not God's plan for all of us, but God does call each and every one of us to proclaim and live the Gospel right where we are. Any one of us can go to participate in community events, visit a neighbor in our congregation who needs help around their house, team up with another church and go into low-income regions and help people with food and property repairs, or offer a ride to someone who needs to go to work or to the doctor. The heart of missions is evangelism, and all of us should do more than talk in our witness of the Lord: we should show it, as well.

- **Go on a short-term mission trip** – I don't really consider week-long mission trips to be complete missionary experiences, but I cannot deny the great experience these type of trips provide into the work of missions and the realities the church faces in other parts of the world. I believe every believer should go on at least one short-term mission trip in their lifetime and see what it is like for those who live the Gospel through their lives in foreign lands.

- **Read about believers in different parts of the world** – Christian experiences are vastly different in different parts of the world. Some Christians experience bitter persecution, torture, and even death due to their faith in Jesus Christ. Many missionaries throughout history laid down their lives in pursuit of the Gospel work. Learn about the church in a bigger picture and the ways that people are serving God all throughout the world, and keep them in prayer.

MISSIONARIES IN HISTORY

Missionary work has been a staple of the church since the early days of Christianity. Take a look at four individuals you may or may not have heard of – and the work they did as missionaries for the Lord.

- **Alopen (Unknown)** – The story of Alopen (perhaps a transliteration of Abraham) is an interesting one in the history of missions, because all we know about him is found in the Nestorian Stele (a tablet that documents the history of early Christianity in China). Alopen was the first recorded missionary to reach China, sometime during the Tang Dynasty. He was a part of the Church of the East (Nestorian Church), and was most likely from the Persian Empire or from Syria. It is believed he was a bishop and appointed the building of many churches.[9]

- **William Carey (1761-1834)** – William Carey was a British Baptist missionary (born in Northamptonshire) who we now call the "father of modern missions." It was an essay he penned that became the foundation for the Baptist Missionary Society. His missions work, done in India, included translation of the Bible into Bengali, Oriya, Assamese, Arabic, Hindi and Sanskrit.[10]

- **Betsey Stockton (c. 1798-1865)** – Born into slavery in New Jersey, Betsey Stockton lived in multiple homes as a slave child, working throughout her childhood. In 1817 she became a member of the First Presbyterian Church in Princeton, New Jersey, and was formally granted her freedom. She remained a maid and through education, also taught. It was at this point in her life she desired to go to Africa as a missionary. She discovered a missions plan at Princeton Theological Seminary to go to Hawaii (back then they were known as the Sandwich Islands) and through a successful application process, became the first single

American woman sent overseas as a missionary in 1822. She later returned to the US in 1825, and then in 1840, helped form the First Presbyterian Church of Color in Princeton (later renamed the Witherspoon Street Church).[11]

- **Gladys May Aylward (1902-1970)** – A hard-working woman who lived her earlier life as a maid, Gladys May Aylward had a desire to work as a missionary from a young age. Turned down because it was believed she could not learn the language, she spent her life savings in 1932 to go to China, crossing Siberia, where she was forced to get off the train and walk the rest of the way to her destination. She worked with another missionary named Jeannie Lawson, and founded The Inn of the Eight Happinesses. She also worked for the Chinese government in an effort to enforce laws against foot binding for young Chinese girls. She became a citizen of China in 1936 and was greatly beloved by the people of China, taking in orphans, adopting them, advocating prison reform, and aiding over one hundred orphans to safety after the Japanese invaded China in 1938.[12]

QUESTIONS AND ANSWERS

- **Can a missionary be a part of the five-fold ministry?**

I believe the ideal situation of a mission team consists of all five offices in the five-fold ministry. While I recognize that this may not always be possible, missionaries have always worked in teams and many throughout history were also a part of an office of the five-fold ministry. It is perfectly acceptable and desirable for a missionary to be an apostle, prophet, evangelist, pastor, or teacher. If one is not a part of the five-fold, they should work in connection with a member of the five-fold, to help train and prepare for missions.

- **Do missionaries have to be licensed and ordained?**

Missionaries must be licensed in accordance with a ministry that supports and encourages their vision for mission work. It is also desirable that a missionary be ordained, especially if they are going on a mission by themselves or without other personnel that may also be ordained. If someone is training to be a missionary or going as a missionary with another minister or other individual who is ordained, then only a license would be required.

- **Are there certain places in the world missionaries should not go?**

If we understand Jesus' commission to make disciples of every nation, then that means missionaries can and should go wherever they are led to go in the world. That having been said, there are many nations that restrict missionary activity or prohibit Christian missionaries.

At current, the top most dangerous nations for Christians are:
  o Laos
  o Uzbekistan
  o Iraq
  o Yemen
  o Maldives
  o Somalia
  o Saudi Arabia
  o Afghanistan
  o Iran
  o North Korea[13]

There are many other nations where the Bible is illegal and Christians face persecution, even though they may not be persecuted as openly as the ten nations listed above. As believers, we recognize the responsibility we have to observe the secular governments (Romans 13:1), and this means that mission work in these countries must be handled within the confines of the laws of these nations. If a missionary feels called to a nation with missionary restrictions, they should learn what they can about the restrictions and the conditions under which they will have to complete their mission.

- **How should someone prepare for missions?**

If someone is interested in missions, they should make sure they have a solid education from a seminary or Bible training program and should learn all they can about the Scriptures, about the nation where they intend to go, about the legal and political process to enter the nation, and about the unique strongholds, challenges, language, culture, economic and beliefs of the people where you intend to minister.

- **If we are not called to serve as missionaries ourselves, how can we be of more assistance to missionaries?**

We all know from emails and social media online how many foreign ministers clamor for our attention and funds if we give them the chance. I have heard of one too many scams involving people claiming to be preachers overseas and ministers over here who give money to these foreign ministers because they think it means they are contributing to missions or covering a foreign ministry. The thing we are missing is the true connection to foreign missions that the church once had. In nations where Christianity is openly practiced without government persecution, the churches, seminaries, and ministries should train, financially support, and support through letters, correspondence and short-term team visits missionaries who go abroad to do the work of ministry.

We should also never forget our command to pray for missions and for missionaries. Every believer should include prayers for missionaries, for people to be called into the mission field, for Christians in other nations (especially where they suffer for their faith) and for the work of missions to increase, especially in this hour.

- **Where do the majority of missionaries come from?**

  According to the different statistical lists that exist about missionaries, the United States still sends out the most missionaries per year; Brazil is second. Other top contenders include Palestine, South Korea, Ireland, Malta, and Samoa.[14]

DISCUSSION, STUDY AND REVIEW QUESTIONS

1. What happened when a city or nation was overthrown by another nation? What happened to citizens in most cases? When the Assyrians overtook the Hebrews, what was unique about that situation? Why did the Assyrians do this?

2. What were the Hebrew priests sent on as a part of this process instituted by the Assyrian government? Where they successful? What does this teach us about missions, and why is it important?

3. What is a missionary? What does the term "missionary" mean? Do missionaries just go into a region to preach? What else do they go to do?

4. What do missionaries reveal to us about the church? Does church work begin and end in local congregations? Why or why not? What did Jesus tell us to do as a part of His Great Commission? What does the work of the missionary remind us about? What must the church do with the Gospel until Jesus returns?

5. Do missionaries always desire their mission? Why do you believe this is? Who is an example of one sent on a mission who did not desire their work? Who is an example of one sent on a mission who did desire their work? Why do you think missionaries respond differently to different missions?

6. How do missionaries operate? How do they receive this divine power? What kind of person is a missionary? How important is service to missionaries, and why is it important?

7. What special ways do missionaries see God work in their lives? What special word do missionaries have for those who are "back home?" What have they seen God do? What do they remind us about?

8. Who is salvation for? What important fact do missionaries remind all of us about? What do missionaries prove by virtue of their work? Why?

9. What are some ways we can encourage and support missionaries?

10. Who were some notable missionaries in history?

11. Discuss and share some of the questions and answers found in the "Questions and Answers" section. What did you learn that you did not know about missionaries? What did you learn that changed your mind about an opinion you might have had prior about missionaries? How did learning about specific issues related to missionaries help you to grow in your understanding of missions? The church? Your own relationship with God?

12. Who is your favorite missionary? Why are they your favorite?

Four ● DREAMER AND VISIONARY

. . . I would stand,
If the night blackened with a coming storm,
Beneath some rock, listening to notes that are
The ghostly language of the ancient earth,
Or make their dim abode in distant winds.
Thence did I drink the visionary power;
And deem not profitless those fleeting moods
Of shadowy exultation: not for this,
That they are kindred to our purer mind
And intellectual life; but that the soul,
Remembering how she felt, but what she felt
Remembering not, retains an obscure sense
Of possible sublimity. . .
– William Wordsworth[1]

THE concept of being a "dreamer" or a "visionary" has long had mixed connotations. Some people think being one who dreams or one with a vision is laudable, while others believe it is fanciful and ridiculous. We've come to associate being a dreamer or a visionary with having many goals and ideals, most of which are laudable, but having no way or ability to bring those goals or dreams to pass. We think of dreamers and visionaries as people who, with the best of intentions, whittle away the time on a cloud of thought and ignorance as they do nothing with their lives.

This is not how the Bible describes dreamers and visionaries. The work of those who have dreams and visions has been considered essential and vital in every era of salvation history, both in the Old and New Testaments. Through dreams and visions, God has conveyed important warnings, information, prophetic details, and purpose to His people. Being one who has a dream or a vision as a Christian is anything but ignorant or lazy!

Learning to recognize true dreams and visions is an important part of being a believer. Being one who has a dream or a vision (or both) helps to piece important aspects of spiritual life together and gives important words to the church, as a whole. I am including both dreams and visions as one function because the two convey the same message (as we will discuss in this chapter) in different forms. These two equally important functions are a way that God is able to reach out to us, through us, and for us, right down until the time when Jesus returns.

TEXT STUDY

Acts 2:14-21

POWER TEXTS

Genesis 15:1-6, Genesis 28:10-22, Genesis 37:5-20, Job 33:8-18, Jeremiah 23:16-22, Daniel 7:1-14, Habakkuk 2:1-3, Matthew 1:18-21, Matthew 2:7-16, Luke 1:5-25, Acts 11:1-18.

POWER VERSE

Acts 2:17:

- *"And it shall come to pass in the last days, saith God, I will pour out of My Spirit upon all flesh: and your sons and daughters shall prophesy, and your young men shall see visions, and your old men shall dream dreams."*

- *"And in the last days it shall be, God declares, that I will pour out My Spirit on all flesh, and your sons and your daughters shall prophesy, and your young men shall see visions, and your old men shall dream dreams."* (ESV)

- *"And it shall come to pass in the last days, says God, that I will pour out My Spirit on all flesh; your sons and your daughters shall prophesy, your young men shall see visions, your old men shall dream dreams."* (PHILLIPS)

- *"And in the last days it will be, God says, that I will pour out My Spirit on all people, and your sons and your daughters will prophesy, and your young men will see visions, and your old men will dream dreams."* (NET)

- *"In the last days, God says, I will pour out My Spirit on all people. Your sons and daughters will prophesy. Your young will see visions. Your elders will dream dreams."* (CEB)

- *"God says: In the last days I will pour out My Spirit on all kinds of people [people; humanity; flesh]. Your sons and daughters will prophesy. Your young men will see visions, your old men will dream dreams."* (EXB)

POWER WORDS

- **Last Days** – From two Greek words: *eschatos* which means, "extreme; the last"[2] and *hemera* which means "the day, used of the natural day, or the interval between sunrise and sunset, as distinguished from and contrasted with the night; of the civil day, or the space of twenty four hours (thus including the night); of the last day of this present age, the day Christ will return from heaven, raise the dead, hold the final judgment, and perfect his kingdom; used of time in general, i.e. the days of his life."[3]

- **Pour out** – From the Greek word *ekcheo* which means "to pour out, shed forth; metaph. to bestow or distribute largely."[4]

- **Spirit** – From the Greek word *pneuma* which means, "a movement of air (a gentle blast); the spirit, i.e. the vital principal by which the body is animated; a spirit, i.e. a simple essence, devoid of all or at least all grosser matter, and possessed of the power of knowing, desiring, deciding, and acting; of God; the disposition or influence which fills and governs the soul of any one."[5]

- **All flesh** – From two Greek words: *pas* which means "individually, each, every, any, all, the whole, everyone, all things, everything; collectively, some of all types"[6] and *sarx* which means "flesh (the soft substance of the living body, which covers the bones and is permeated with blood) of both man and beasts; the body; a living creature (because possessed of a body of flesh) whether man or beast; the flesh, denotes mere human nature, the earthly nature of man apart from divine influence, and therefore prone to sin and opposed to God."[7]

- **Sons and daughters** – From two Greek words: *huios* which means, "a son; son of man; son of God"[8] and *thugater* which means "a daughter."[9]

- **Prophesy** – From the Greek word *propheteuo* which means "to prophesy, to be a prophet, speak forth by divine inspirations, to predict, to prophesy, with the idea of foretelling future events pertaining esp. to the kingdom of God, to utter forth, declare, a thing which can only be known by divine revelation, to break forth under sudden impulse in lofty discourse or praise of the divine counsels, under like prompting, to teach, refute, reprove, admonish, comfort others, to act as a prophet, discharge the prophetic office."[10]

- **Young men** – From the Greek word *neaniskos* which means "a young man, youth."[11]

- **Visions** – From the Greek word *horasis* which means, "the act of seeing; appearance, visible form; a vision, an appearance divinely granted in an ecstasy or dream."[12]

- **Old men** – From the Greek word *presbuteros* which means "elder, of age; a term of rank or office."[13]

- **Dreams** – From the Greek word *enupniazomai* which means "to dream (divinely suggested) dreams; metaph., to be beguiled with sensual images and carried away to an impious course of conduct."[14]

HISTORICAL CONTEXT

Church history has branded Pentecost as the "birthday of the church." This means that on Pentecost in 33 AD, the church was officially born because the Spirit of God, the Holy Spirit. On Pentecost, we see the prophecy that in the times of the church, in the last era of understood history before Jesus comes back, that the Spirit would be poured out upon all people. This is in contrast to the history of salvation to this point, where it was exclusively offered through the Jewish people. Now a new day is born that opens up salvation to everyone, anywhere they are, who will call on and believe in Jesus Christ. To confirm, God sends signs of His Spirit upon all people manifest in different signs and wonders.

NOTES ON TEXT

Two of the signs and wonders God promises to pour out are dreams and visions. While they did happen in the Old Testament, they appear to have been rare, and were often most common among individuals who were prophets. In the New Testament, however, dreams and visions are open to the young and the old, of every nation, tongue, and tribe. Clearly God has something to say, and He wants to say it to as many people as possible. One of the ways He will say these things to humanity is through the outpouring of His Spirit in the form of dreams and visions.

POWER POINTS

- Dreams and visions are powerful ways in which God communicates with people to convey a prophetic message (Habakkuk 2:1-3). They operate by a similar means: both appear in a visionary or picture form, in which the individual is able to see and perceive the message by sight and hearing, and both seem tangibly real to the individual who receives them. The only difference between a dream and a message is that a dream happens when one is asleep, while a vision happens when one is awake. The message of the dream and vision may be scary or comforting, but always alerts the dreamer or visionary to something that is coming, something to which they need to pay attention, something they need to do, or something to help keep them away from wrongdoing and preserve them from danger (Job 33:8-18).

- Dreams and visions are available to all people, anywhere in the world, old or young, even male or female. God has promised that He would pour His Spirit out, and His people would prophesy as a result of their dreams and visions. They are a part of the signs and wonders of the age, and the end result of such true prophecies is that anyone who genuinely believes and calls upon the Name of the Lord will be saved (Acts 2:14-21).

- Dreams and visions alike tend to be largely symbolic (Genesis 37:5-20, Daniel 7:1-14). In terms of waking understanding, they do not always make logical sense to our minds and to our levels of reasoning. In fact, at times, they can seem downright odd or strange. It often takes interpretation to understand the world of dreams and visions, to understand the unique symbols that go along with dreams and visions, and recognizing the way that God seeks to speak to us through dreams and visions.

- Sometimes dreams and visions reveal something essential about the person themselves, such as relates to their destiny or their calling in life (Genesis 15:1-6, Luke 1:5-25). They are not always easy to accept, nor are they always things that have a fulfillment totally in one person's lifetime. Many dreams and visions have a double meaning: they relate to something that person will experience, but also to a deeper spiritual depth that the person cannot see right then and there (Genesis 28:10-22).

- Dreams and visions can also warn about things to come if people make different decisions or if they remain where they are. Joseph had a dream informing him about Mary's pregnancy with Jesus, and a dream about fleeing to Egypt to escape Herod's massacre of all the boys under two years old (Matthew 1:18-21, Matthew 2:13-16). The Magi also had a dream, warning them to return to their own country on a route that would defy Herod (Matthew 2:1-12). Obedience to these visions changed the course of history, and could have easily altered it in another direction if the warnings present within them had not been heeded.

- Dreams and visions also point individuals to a greater obedience toward their destiny. It is through dreams and visions that our spiritual worlds are expanded, and thus our understanding and perspective this side of heaven also changes and increases. In the New Testament, we see the vital role that dreams and visions played in the movement and activity of the first church leaders, because the early church leaders needed their vision expanded as they launched the church into its Kingdom role in all nations. This example should call us to attention: visions and dreams helped them to be humbled, not proud. Through true dreams and visions, we find ourselves humbled before God, and in awe of our place in His plan.

- The Bible reminds us that dreams and visions are complicated things, and not every dream and vision we have are all about something spiritual or some deeper thing in life. It is very possible to take something away from a dream or vision that is false or misleading, and it is possible to follow false teaching as a result of a false vision (Jeremiah 23:16-22). As with all things spiritual, we must remain humble, teachable, and open to accurate and true interpretation.

WAYS TO TELL IF A DREAM OR VISION IS RELEVANT

I remember someone telling me a long time ago that whenever we are sleeping, we are always dreaming, even if we don't remember our dreams. This means that having a dream we remember is a pretty rare thing in and of itself. This does not mean, however, that every single dream or vision we have is from God, and that every dream or vision we have rates attention or time in interpretation. Here are a few ways that you can tell if a dream or vision is worthy of further interpretation.

- **It doesn't meet the description of the typical run-of-the-mill dreams and visions** – Our dream states and vision states are affected by the stories, news pieces, and other things (especially audio and visual things) that demand our time and command our attention. This means that we are easily influenced by news items that we see over and over again. I cannot count the number of people who come and tell me they've had a vision or a dream that seems to be circulating among people forever and ever: New York City being destroyed by a tidal wave, the east coast of the United States plummeting under water, the United States being invaded by various Islamic attacks…you can get the picture. These dreams and visions are highly influenced by the number of suggestions, impressions, and other people who have either taught on these things (and some of them go back centuries, believe me) or somehow hinted at them. Throw in a few news stories or sensationalist posts on the internet, and you've got yourself a subconscious dream or visual state that has been completely concocted by what you watch and absorb during waking hours. The dreams and visions people had in the Bible were odd or different, especially in symbolism. They didn't make sense when they came to consciousness and they didn't sound right when they told them to someone else. In other words: they were odd. They weren't dreams or visions that a bunch of other people had, even though other people might have had dreams or visions. If a dream seems particularly unique to you, has symbolism you don't readily understand, or makes you go "Hmmmmm..." it is a dream or vision you should pay attention to.

- **You know the dream contains a lot of symbols –** Symbolism is one of those things that tends to be unique to the one who has the dream or the vision. Yes, sometimes dreams and visions are clear to the one that receives them, but sometimes they aren't very clear or understandable. If you recognize a dream or vision to be symbolic (even if you aren't sure what all the symbols mean, it is probably something that is pointing you to something else.

- **The dream somehow changes you, even if you don't understand all the changes that are associated with it –** Prophetic or visionary dreams or visions are always about some sort of change: either a change within the individual, a change to come in a larger sense (as in society or the church), a revelation of some sort of destiny, or an essential warning of some sort. Some dreams and visions are a combination of all of these things. If a change comes from your dream or vision, it is most likely a dream or vision that merits attention.

DREAMERS AND VISIONARIES IN HISTORY

As we can see from the Bible, people have had dreams and visions since the beginning of time. Even though we don't always hear about it in church history or from the pulpit, people have had dreams and visions all throughout the history of the church, as well. Here are some dreamers and visionaries that you may or may not know about, and the way that their dreams and visions impacted us, right down to the present day.

- **Perpetua (d. 203)** – We don't know much about the lives of Perpetua and Felicity, except that they were the quintessential "ride or die" story of early Christianity. Perpetua was a noblewoman, and Felicity was her servant. Both were martyred under the decree of Septimius Severus, a Roman emperor in the early 200s. It was Perpetua who asked for and received a vision (climbing a dangerous ladder to which various weapons were attached, with a dragon at the foot of the ladder), and the vision clarified for her that those imprisoned would become martyrs, and they would suffer. Her vision did indeed come to pass, and the martyrs were killed.[15]

- **Catherine of Siena (1347-1380)** – A Dominican nun, Catherine of Siena was also a philosopher, a scholastic, and a theologian. She was known throughout her life for her cheerful disposition, and, according to accounts, started having visions of Jesus Christ when she was around five or six years old. By the time she was seven, she vowed to give her entire life over to God and to His will. Even though some of her visions seem odd or strange to many of us (especially by modern standards), Catherine's visions helped to give her fortitude and persist in a life devoted to the Lord, despite the fact that her family desired her to take other worldly paths unto success. She was known for instructing followers and also involved herself in advocating for clerical reform and renewal. She spent most of her life in a state of rigorous fasting and strict adherence to structure and spent much of her later life preaching, praying, teaching, and advocating peace. To this day, she is considered a highly respected figure for her different writings.[16]

- **Martin Luther (1483-1546)** – Most people have heard of Martin Luther, whose study and stance on many essential things led to the Protestant Reformation and the foundation of the Lutheran Church. Martin Luther was a monk who spent his early life in education and scholarship, later devoted to the Augustinian order, spending most of his time in prayer and fasting. After discovering the work of the Roman Catholic Church in his day did not align with the teachings of the Bible, he sought to bring about reformation, but all he wound up doing was finding himself excommunicated from the church. His life then consisted of theological training, teaching, and the start of a new church for any and all who were ready for a change. What many do not know is Martin Luther also experienced visions in his life, especially of apocalyptic and end times scenarios. He his lauded throughout history for his brave and bold stance, and for transforming Christian history forever.[17]

- **John Bosco (1815-1888)** – John Bosco had an interesting experience with dreams: he didn't take his seriously enough. He had been having them since he was nine years old, and they explained great detail to him about God's will for his life. Even though he knew that dreams and visions were accepted aspects of church doctrine, he was highly skeptical of what God had to say to him through his dreams and his encounters with God in his dreams. It did not help that his family laughed at the dreams he was having and that his friends thought he was mentally ill! Through his dreams, John Bosco learned he was to help and care for neglected and abandoned boys in his lifetime, both physically and spiritually, and he did just that, until his death at age seventy-two.[18]

QUESTIONS AND ANSWERS

- **Can we do anything to bring on a dream or a vision?**

I have heard of people doing all sorts of things in an attempt to hear from God or have a dream or vision: everything from fasting from food and water, to intense and long prayer sessions, to self-abuse or refraining from sleep.

  All of these probably sound like super-spiritual things we can do to try and get God's attention and somehow make Him realize we want something incredible to come our way. It's great to think we will follow the footsteps of the ancients and do something with even more fervor and extremism to get the same – or better – results. With dreams and visions, however, it doesn't quite work like this. I think that within moderation, fasting and prayer can be great things to help us prepare to hear from God and bring us to a deeper place in Him. The reality about dreams and visions, however, is that they don't work like this. When God knows we are ready to have a dream or a vision, He gives it to us. It's not a state we can genuinely induce and believe that the experience we have is truly from God. God either gives the dream or the vision, or He does not.

- **Is there one type of person more likely to have a dream or a vision than someone else?**

Not really. Even though Old Testament prophets frequently had dreams and visions as a part of their prophetic office, we see many people in Bible history who had dreams and visions and were not, according to office nor definition, prophets themselves. God can speak to anyone through a dream or a vision, which is part of what makes dreams and visions so important as functions. Individuals in the five-fold or the appointments are no more likely to have a dream or a vision than someone else.

- **What should I do if I have a dream or a vision and I am not sure about it?**

In the next chapter, we are going to discuss dream interpretation, because interpreting dreams (and by extension, visions) is also a function of the church. If you have a dream or a vision and you are not sure what it means, it is essential that you speak to someone that is discerned to genuinely have the ability to interpret dreams and visions. This is not something that comes from reading a book, nor is it something that can be studied. For this reason, a trusted interpreter of dreams and visions is the one to speak with when you are not sure as to what dreams and visions may mean. You can also pray and ask God to reveal the nature of the dream to you, directly, if you don't find the answers you seek in an interpreter.

- **I know someone who claims to have had a vision, and they are arrogant about it. Was it a genuine vision?**

True visions should humble us before God, and cause us to be in awe of all things that relate to spirituality. Because visions often relate to the spiritual world and go beyond natural revelations of things, they shouldn't cause us to become puffed up and arrogant within ourselves. If someone had a vision and now they are arrogant or conceited about it, it is either a false vision, or has been interpreted in a way that is false.

- **Can a dream or vision be from God, but be interpreted falsely?**

  Yes, although the results will most likely be the same as if it was a false vision all together. Improper interpretation can cause whatever God intends to convey through a dream or vision to be lost and for people to follow false teachings and adhere to a false vision. Discernment is highly important on matters of dreams and visions.

- **What does a dream or a vision look and feel like?**

  Most experiences of dreams and visions do vary between people, but most report an awareness of being in the place of the dream or vision, even if it is to watch what is going on. They also report with vivid detail things such as colors, sounds, symbols (even if they are not understood to be symbols or understood properly) and a feeling of being outside of themselves. Some report feeling as if they are somehow outside of time.

DISCUSSION, STUDY AND REVIEW QUESTIONS

1. What has history branded Pentecost? What does this mean? What do we see in Pentecost? How does this become a new day in salvation history? How does God confirm this new day?

2. What are two of the signs and wonders God promises to pour out? Who most commonly experienced dreams and visions in the Old Testament? Who can receive them in the New Testament? What is one of the ways God will say what He has to unto humanity?

3. What are dreams and visions? What is similar about dreams and visions? What is the main difference between a dream

and a vision? What kind of messages come through dreams and visions?

4. Who can receive dreams and visions? What are they a part of? What is the end result of dreams and visions?

5. What can dreams and visions reveal about a person? Are they always easy to accept? What double message is usually found in a dream or vision that relates to an individual?

6. Can dreams and visions warn people about things to come? What are some examples of such dreams as we find in the Bible? Why is obedience to such dreams important?

7. How do dreams and visions point us toward our greater destiny? How does our perception of things change through dreams and visions? What role did dreams and visions play in the movement of early church leaders? What do true visions help us to be as people?

8. Are dreams and visions complicated? Does every dream or vision have a deeper meaning? Is it possible to take something false from a dream or vision? How can we avoid this?

9. What are some ways we can tell if a dream or vision is relevant?

10. Who were some notable dreamers and visionaries in history?

11. Discuss and share some of the questions and answers found in the "Questions and Answers" section. What did you learn that you did not know about dreamers and visionaries? What did you learn that changed your mind about an opinion you might have had prior about dreamers and visionaries? How did learning about specific issues

related to dreamers and visionaries help you to grow in your understanding of dreams and visions? The church? Your own relationship with God?

12. Who is your favorite dreamer or visionary? Why are they your favorite?

Five ● INTERPRETER OF DREAMS AND VISIONS

As everyone knows, the ancients before Aristotle did not consider the dream a product of the dreaming mind, but a divine inspiration, and in ancient times the two antagonistic streams, which one finds throughout in the estimates of dream life, were already noticeable. They distinguished between true and valuable dreams, sent to the dreamer to warn him or to foretell the future, and vain, fraudulent, and empty dreams, the object of which was to misguide or lead him to destruction.
— Sigmund Freud[1]

"COME to dream interpretation class!" "Learn my sure-fire way to interpret dreams!" "Learn about the intricacies of dream prophecy!" "Come and learn how to interpret visions!" We've all seen the headlines and event invites online, posted by people of various ministries and affiliations calling people to come out and take their class (usually for money) to learn how to "interpret dreams and visions." Numerous big-name leaders have written books that encode dreams and the different symbols present in dreams and visions, sometimes in complicated ways, and sometimes quite simply.

It's obvious from history that dreams have puzzled and intrigued people since the beginning of time. For thousands of years, people have had dreams and visions, and know they were a message of some kind, even if they don't understand what the message is. For this very reason, God has given different individuals the ability to interpret, or explain, the different symbols and situations that present themselves in dreams and visions. While not all dreams and visions contain a message from God, a dream and vision interpreter has the ability to explain a dream or vision that is from God and does so by the power of God.

TEXT STUDY

Daniel 5:1-31

POWER TEXTS

Genesis 40:1-23, Genesis 41:1-40, Judges 7:13-21, Jeremiah 27:8-15, Daniel 2:1-49. Daniel 4:1-37, Daniel 7:1-14, Daniel 8:1-27.

POWER VERSE

Daniel 5:12:

- *"Forasmuch as an excellent spirit, and knowledge, and understanding, interpreting of dreams, and shewing of hard sentences, and dissolving of doubts, were found in the same Daniel, whom the king named Belteshazzar: now let Daniel be called, and he will shew the interpretation."*

- *"He also changed the man's name from Daniel to Belteshazzar. Not only is he wise and intelligent, but he can explain dreams and riddles and solve difficult problems. Send for Daniel, and he will tell you what the writing means."* (CEV)

- *"This man Daniel, whom the king named Belteshazzar, has exceptional ability and is filled with divine knowledge and understanding. He can interpret dreams, explain riddles, and solve difficult problems. Call for Daniel, and he will tell you what the writing means."* (NLT)

- *"Because an excellent spirit, knowledge, and understanding to interpret dreams, explain riddles, and solve problems were found in this Daniel, whom the king named Belteshaz'zar. Now let Daniel be called, and he will show the interpretation."* (RSV)

- *"This man Daniel, whom the king called Belteshazzar, was found to have a keen mind and knowledge and understanding, and also the ability to interpret dreams, explain riddles and solve difficult problems. Call for Daniel, and he will tell you what the writing means."* (NIV)

- *"Because an excellent spirit, knowledge, and understanding to interpret dreams, clarify riddles, and solve knotty problems were found in this same Daniel, whom the king named Belteshazzar. Now let Daniel be called, and he will show the interpretation."* (AMP)

POWER WORDS

- **Excellent spirit** – From two Aramaic words: *yattiyr* which means, "pre-eminent, surpassing, extreme, extraordinary; exceedingly, extremely"[2] and *ruwach* which means "spirit, wind."[3]

- **Knowledge** – From the Aramaic word *manda`* which means "knowledge, power of knowing."[4]

- **Understanding** – From the Aramaic word *soklethanuw* which means, "insight."[5]

- **Interpreting of dreams** – From two Aramaic words: *peshar* which means "to interpret"[6] and *chelem* which means "dream."[7]

- **Shewing of hard sentences** – From two Aramaic words: 'achavah which means, "declaration, a declaring"[8] and 'achiydah which means "puzzle, riddle."[9]

- **Dissolving of doubts** – From two Aramaic words: shere' which means "to loosen, abide, begin"[10] and qetar which means "knot, joint, problem."[11]

- **Found** – From the Aramaic word shekach which means "to find."[12]

- **Daniel** – From the Aramaic word Daniye'l which means, "God is my judge; the 4th of the greater prophets, taken as hostage in the first deportation to Babylon, because of the gift of God of the interpretation of dreams, he became the 2nd in command of the Babylon empire and lasted through the end of the Babylonian empire and into the Persian empire. His prophecies are the key to the understanding of end time events. Noted for his purity and holiness by contemporary prophet, Ezekiel."[13]

- **Belteshazzar** – From the Aramaic word Beltesha'tstsar which means "Belteshazzar = lord of the straitened's treasure; the 4th of the greater prophets, taken as hostage in the first deportation to Babylon; because of the gift of God of the interpretation of dreams, he became the 2nd in command of the Babylon empire and lasted through the end of the Babylonian empire and into the Persian empire. His prophecies are the key to the understanding of end time events. Noted for his purity and holiness by contemporary prophet, Ezekiel."[14]

- **Interpretation** – From the Aramaic word peshar which means "interpretation (of dream)."[15]

HISTORICAL CONTEXT

Belshazzar's image in Biblical history sounds much like the role of many foreign kings, and much like the image of Babylon many Bible readers have: stories of conquer, excess, idolatry, oppression, and intimidation. Belshazzar had a special experience, however, warning him that his days of leadership were coming to an end, very quickly. Later that very night, he died, in connection with the warning. Let this be a warning to all of us that in history, no matter how assured we may be of a leader or where someone is, untamed behavior always comes to an end.

NOTES ON TEXT

Even though the message on the wall was for Belshazzar and he was the one who had the vision experience, he couldn't understand it. The symbolism and the words did not mean much to him, because he was not in a place of clarity in his life to understand what it would mean. Notably shook up by the situation, he wanted it clarified for him so he could understand it. Daniel was called, because he was noted for being a balanced individual who had the ability to interpret dreams and handle complex issues that were also presented to him. Not just being a monotone individual, Daniel's work as an interpreter of dreams and visions shows our relevant dreams and visions to be more than just encoded messages, but revelations to us from God in the form of complex characters and ideals.

POWER POINTS

- In reviewing a little of what we spoke of in the last chapter, dreams and visions are powerful ways that God communicates with people. Recognizing that dreams and visions alike are largely symbolic, sometimes the meaning of a dream or vision is not clear to the one who received it (Genesis 40:1-8, Daniel 5:1-12). In this instance, someone who can interpret the dream or vision will be able to hear the situations of the dream or vision, ask questions accordingly, and provide an interpretation of the dream or vision's contents.

- Dream and vision interpretation is not something that can be taught from a book. Because dreams and visions can be specific to the individuals who receive them or generalized in a larger sense, the symbolism present in dreams and visions may mean different things in different situations. Sometimes symbolism may represent something important or meaningful to the person who had the dream or vision, and it won't have that same understanding to someone else who also has that symbol in a dream or vision. For this reason, believers should be very wary of individuals who try to "teach" dream or vision interpretation. The Bible is clear that interpretations come from God, not from being able to look up symbols in a book (Genesis 40:1-23, Genesis 41:1-40).

- Dream and vision interpreters are individuals who are able to explain complicated matters. They are people who can figure out problems, who are well-rounded in knowledge, who have many experiences, and who know the power of learning and understanding. While we know that interpretations belong to God, knowing about the world and about complex things shows an ability to understand symbols and other complexities that come forth in dreams and visions (Daniel 5:1-16).

- There are times when sometimes people can interpret their own dreams and visions, or when God may directly reveal the meaning of a dream or a vision to an individual. Having the vision or dream and interpreting can also be a very exhausting experience, because it drains of spiritual power. While dream interpretation appears easy on the surface or to come to an individual with ease, it is something that can seem puzzling to a dream interpreter in the natural realm. That is what proves interpretations come from God, and not that person (Daniel 8:1-27).

- Dreams and visions do not always bring with them a fun or an uplifting message. Some dreams and visions bring serious interpretations and serious sights (Daniel 4:1-37, Daniel 7:1-14). If a dream or vision is interpreted improperly, it should not be heeded. Sometimes dreams and visions are exciting, sometimes they are serious, sometimes they are warnings, sometimes they serve correction, and sometimes they are encouragements. A true dream and vision interpreter knows the difference (Daniel 5:17-31, Jeremiah 27:8-15).

- Every true dream and vision interpreter praises God for the revelation that comes forth through the interpretation. They do not call on false divination methods, and stand strong in the face where traditional means of divination fail and falter. When no one else has the answer, one that has the necessary revelation from God to interpret dreams and visions will be able to stand, even if the results of the interpretation are not well accepted (Daniel 2:1-49).

- Hearing the interpretation of a dream or vision should always bring the recipient to a place of destiny and dedication (Judges 7:13-21). Even though not every dream or vision is personal to the individual, knowing that God has revealed something that is important enough for a dream or a vision. This means dream and vision interpretation is a part of understanding God's revelation to us as we receive and prophesy in part, this side of heaven.

GUIDELINES FOR SEEKING OUT A DREAM AND VISION INTERPRETER

When it comes to dream and vision interpretations, there is a never-ending parade of people who are more than eager to "interpret" it for you. The problem is that not every interpreter does so by the power of God, and not every individual who interprets does so correctly. This means if you have a dream or vision that you are genuinely uncertain about, you need to find someone who can genuinely interpret. Here are some general guidelines for assessing the true from the false when it comes to dream and vision interpretation.

- **Don't put a "blast" out on social media, hoping someone will offer you an interpretation** – I know that it is tempting to try and solicit as much help as is feasible when in a confused state, but posting a dream online and then asking if anyone has an interpretation is asking for multiple interpretations that, will most likely, confuse and contradict one another.

- **Don't tell everyone you know about it** – Paralleling what I said about blasting it on social media, telling everyone you know about your dream or vision may not just be unwise from an interpretive point, it is also unwise to expose yourself to everyone you know, in general. Sometimes it is hard to tell who is really for us from who is not, and allowing everyone such personal access to the words God is speaking to you is not always wise.

- **If you do not know a dream or vision interpreter personally, ask your leader if they can recommend someone** – Not all of us know people who can properly interpret dreams and visions. In fact, I would put interpretation of dreams and visions in the category of things that are on the rare side, meaning not everyone who thinks they have it really does. If you don't have someone you can directly go to, it is best to ask your spiritual leader if they know of someone you can talk to about your dream or vision in order to get a clear and proper perspective on what God is saying through your dream or vision.

VERSES IN THE SCRIPTURES THAT APPLY TO DREAM INTERPRETATION

Because we know dreams and visions have been going on throughout history, that also means people have always been needed to interpret dreams and visions. That having been said, it is almost impossible to find a dream or vision interpreter who was specifically known for that throughout history. That doesn't mean that the Scriptures do not give us wise counsel when it comes to dream interpretation. Here are some Scriptural words about dream and vision interpretation.

- **Ecclesiastes 5:2** – *For a dream comes with much business, and a fool's voice with many words.* (ESV) In other words: dreams come with many cares, or with many burdens. Those burdens and cares can either be because we genuinely don't understand what God is saying to us through them, or they can be because we are over-interpreting meaning into them. The Bible is clear that we should be cautious when it comes to reading too much meaning into dreams, and we should keep a balance when it comes to interpretation.

- **Matthew 1:20** – *But as he considered these things, behold, an angel of the Lord appeared to him in a dream, saying, "Joseph, son of David, do not fear to take Mary as your wife, for that which is conceived in her is from the Holy Spirit."* (ESV)This is a dream that came with its own built-in interpretation for time's sake. Joseph didn't have time to interpret a lot of complicated symbols or to go find someone who could, so God set forth in the dream to make sure Joseph got word from an angel who interpreted it for him in the dream itself.

- **Genesis 40:8** – *They said to him, "We have had dreams, and there is no one to interpret them." And Joseph said to them,*

"Do not interpretations belong to God? Please tell them to me." (ESV) True dream and vision interpretation comes forth from God and the true interpreter, knowing this fact, is not afraid to ask when a dream situation comes up. Knowing whether it is from God or not, the interpreter can work, accordingly.

- **Jeremiah 29:8** – *For thus says the LORD of Hosts, the God of Israel: Do not let your prophets and your diviners who are among you deceive you, and do not listen to the dreams that they dream.* (ESV) Don't allow dreams, false dreams, dreams that sound good, visions that sound 'trendy' or the words of hollow, empty people deceive you when it comes to the balance of dream and vision interpretation, and the important understanding that comes therein.

QUESTIONS AND ANSWERS

- **What happens when I receive a conflicting interpretation on a dream or vision?**

Conflicting interpretations of dreams and visions comes from exposing your dream or vision to too many different people. For this reason, as I stated earlier, I do not recommend asking multiple people for interpretation of a dream. If you have already done that and now you are faced with many people telling you different things, I have found that many interpretations somehow resonate as a confirmation of something God is already speaking to us about or has already revealed to us in the past, and it tends to be easy to see if a dream or vision interpretation resonates with something in our spirit that God has already made clear in another way. If one interpretation stands out in this way more so than another does, then that can help clarify confusion. If you are still unsure, it is possible none of the interpretations really hit on the essence of the dream or vision. In this instance, pray, talk to a spiritual leader, and ask for revelation about the dream or vision at hand.

- **Is there any aspect to dream and vision interpretation that can benefit from research?**

While interpretations belong to God, it is notable that the dream and vision interpreter is an individual that is familiar with many things and knowledgeable about many complex subjects. We gain understanding through exposure to many things and by knowing the world around us. By learning about God's world and proper scholarship of our world, we are better able to understand how He moves throughout humanity, and what He is saying to us through dreams and visions today.

- **What should I do if I receive a dream or vision interpretation and I am not sure about it?**

I believe it is vital to pray and connect with people who have genuine abilities, especially in a church where everyone thinks they are everything, all the time. If you receive an interpretation that you are just not sure about, pray about it, talk about it with a leader or someone else that you trust, and seek clarity. If you know the individual who provided the interpretation to be one who is able to function as a dream and vision interpreter, then ask them for clarification on the interpretation if that is an option.

- **Will a dream or vision interpreter have an interpretation for every dream and vision they hear about?**

Because functions arise as necessary, I do not believe a dream or vision interpreter has the ability to answer every single dream or vision that comes their way, every single time. There are times when an interpreter may be tired, may be off their game, or may be nothing more than not the individual who is supposed to bring forth the fullness of the vision or dream at hand. A true interpreter will admit they do not have the answer, and can either pray about it, or recommend you talk to someone else who has the genuine gift and is able to provide the answers you seek.

- **Do you believe dream and vision interpretation is the same as it was for people in the Bible?**

The purpose of dreams and visions in the Bible was to convey important messages to people. The purpose of interpretation is to make sure that the message within the dreams and visions was received and properly understood. If this is the purpose of dreams and visions and interpretation of both, then the purpose is exactly the same. Even though the form and some of the symbolism of dreams and visions might be different today (as times have changed and things that were familiar to the ancients aren't always the same for us today), the bottom-line purpose of these vital functions remain the same and will remain the same, until the time when Jesus returns.

- **Does every dream or vision we have require interpretation?**

No. Sometimes a dream or a vision is just a dream or a vision, and doesn't require interpretation because there is no message within either one to explain or clarify. A true interpreter knows the difference between a dream or a vision with a message and a dream or a vision without a message.

DISCUSSION, STUDY AND REVIEW QUESTIONS

1. What do we know of Belshazzar's image in the Bible? What special experience did Belshazzar have? What warning do all of us find in Belshazzar's experience?

2. Could Belshazzar explain the experience he had? Why did the symbolism and words not mean much to him? Why was Daniel called in to the situation? Why was Daniel a special choice for this task?

3. What are dreams and visions? What do dreams and visions often contain? Why are these symbols not readily understood? What does someone who is a dream and vision interpreter do?

4. Can dream and vision interpretation be taught from a book? Why or why not? Should we caution those who try to "teach" dream and vision interpretation? Why or why not? Who do interpretations come from?

5. What kind of individuals are dream and vision interpreters? What else can they do? How do these different things relate to dream and vision interpretation?

6. Can people ever interpret their own dreams and visions? What are some circumstances that arise that would require this? Is having a dream or vision and interpreting it an exhausting experience? Why or why not? Do dreams and visions always make sense to an interpreter in the natural realm? Why or why not?

7. Are dreams and visions always uplifting? Why or why not? Should a dream or vision improperly interpreted be heeded? Why or why not? What kinds of visions and dreams are there? Does a true interpreter know the difference?

8. Who does a true dream and vision interpreter praise for interpretation and revelation? Do they call on divination methods? Why or why not? When no one else has the answer, will a true interpreter have the answer?

9. What should dream and vision interpretation always do for us? What is understanding dream and vision interpretation a part of? Why is it important?

10. What are some guidelines for seeking out a dream and vision interpreter?

11. What are some verses in the Bible that apply to dream and vision interpretation? What are they saying to us?

12. Discuss and share some of the questions and answers found in the "Questions and Answers" section. What did you learn that you did not know about dream and vision interpreters? What did you learn that changed your mind about an opinion you might have had prior about dream and vision interpreters? How did learning about specific issues related to dream and vision interpreters help you to grow in your understanding of dreams and vision interpretation? The church? Your own relationship with God?

13. Who is your favorite dream or vision interpreter? Why are they your favorite?

Six ● INTERCESSOR

We never know how God will answer our prayers, but we can expect that He will get us involved in His plan for the answer. If we are true intercessors, we must be ready to take part in God's work on behalf of the people for whom we pray.
– Corrie Ten Boom[1]

IF you are a part of ministry today or have any ministry presence on the internet, it seems like everyone is quick to call themselves an "intercessor." If you inquire or look closely at their claims, you will find that all of them do something different. Many who call themselves "intercessors" are people who pray for other people, but is that a correct definition of intercession? Is intercession just a matter of prayer? Some people who are intercessors also consider themselves to be prophets, but are prophets always intercessors? Is intercession a part of being a prophet, or is it something else? With so many opinions about intercession, what exactly does it mean to be an intercessor?

As with the rest of the things we are discussing in this book, being an intercessor is a function of the church. Unfortunately, due to sensationalism of the issue, most people in church today do not understand the proper role and work of an intercessor. While it does involve prayer, elements of the prophetic, and an intense dedication to see things through, intercession is not any of the things that we hear people describe it as being. In looking at intercession for real, it will help us to better understand this essential function – and why true intercession is so severely lacking in today's church.

TEXT STUDY

1 Timothy 2:1-7

POWER TEXTS

Genesis 18:16-33, Job 16:15-22, Isaiah 53:6-12, Isaiah 59:11-16, Jeremiah 7:15-20, Jeremiah 27:17-22, Jeremiah 36:20-26, Romans 8:26-30, Romans 11:1-5, Hebrews 7:22-28.

POWER VERSE

1 Timothy 2:1-2:

- *"I exhort therefore, that, first of all, supplications, prayers, intercessions, and giving of thanks, be made for all men; for kings, and for all that are in authority; that we may lead a quiet and peaceable life in all godliness and honesty."*

- *"First of all, then I tell [urge; exhort] you to pray for all people, asking God for what they need and being thankful to Him [make petitions, prayers, intercessions, and thanksgivings for all people]. Pray for rulers [kings] and for all who have authority so that we can have quiet and peaceful lives full of worship and respect for God [in all godliness and dignity/reverence]."* (EXB)

- *"Here then is my charge: First, supplications, prayers, intercessions and thanksgivings should be made on behalf of all men: for kings and rulers in positions of responsibility, so that our common life may be lived in peace and quiet, with a proper sense of God and of our responsibility to Him for what we do with our lives."* (PHILLIPS)

- *"First of all, then, I urge that supplications, prayers, intercessions, and thanksgivings be made for all people, for kings and all who are in high positions, that we may lead a peaceful and quiet life, godly and dignified in every way."* (ESV)

- *"I exhort, then, first of all, there be made supplications, prayers, intercessions, thanksgivings, for all men: for kings, and all who are in authority, that a quiet and peaceable life we may lead in all piety and gravity."* (YLT)

- *"First of all, then, I admonish and urge that petitions, prayers, intercessions, and thanksgivings be offered on behalf of all men, for kings and all who are in positions of authority or high responsibility, that [outwardly] we may pass a quiet and undisturbed life [and inwardly] a peaceable one in all godliness and reverence and seriousness in every way."* (AMP)

POWER WORDS

- **Exhort** – From the Greek word *parakaleo* which means, "to call to one's side, call for, summon; to address, speak to, (call to, call upon), which may be done in the way of exhortation, entreaty, comfort, instruction, etc."[2]

- **First** – From the Greek word *proton* which means "first in time or place; first in rank; first, at the first."[3]

- **Supplications** – From the Greek word *deesis* which means "need, indigence, want, privation, penury; a seeking, asking, entreating, entreaty to God or to man."[4]

- **Prayers** – From the Greek word *proseuche* which means, "prayer addressed to God; a place set apart or suited for the offering of prayer."[5]

- **Intercessions** – From the Greek word *enteuxis* which means, "a falling in with, meeting with."[6]

- **Giving of thanks** – From the Greek word *eucharistia* which means, "thankfulness; the giving of thanks."[7]

- **All men** – From two Greek words: *pas* which means "individually; each, every, any, all, the whole, everyone, all things, everything; collectively, some of all types"[8] and *anthropos* which means "a human being, whether male or female; indefinitely, someone, a man, one; in the plural, people; joined with other words, merchantman."[9]

- **Kings** – From the Greek word *basileus* which means, "leader of the people, prince, commander, lord of the land, king."[10]

- **Authority** – From the Greek word *huperoche* which means "elevation, pre-eminence, superiority; metaph. excellence."[11]

- **Quiet** – From the Greek word *eremos* which means "quiet, tranquil."[12]

- **Peaceable** – From the Greek word *hesuchios* which means "quiet, tranquil."[13]

- **Life** - From the Greek word *bios* which means "life."[14]

- **Godliness** – From the Greek word *eusebeia* which means "reverence, respect; piety towards God, godliness."[15]

- **Honesty** – From the Greek word *semnotes* which means "the characteristic of a thing or person which entitles to reverence and respect, dignity, majesty, sanctity; honour, purity."[16]

HISTORICAL CONTEXT

People throughout history have always known to call on their own needs and voice their own issues before they issue those of others. The Apostle Paul, however, advises the believers to pray differently, and, in an indirect way, pray that their own needs are met. The injunction to make supplications, pray, intercede, and give thanks first for all people, and then lift up prayers for governing officials ensured that the believers would be able to live peaceable lives, not disruptive of anyone, worshipping without hindrance, anywhere they may be in the world. Even though the politics don't always line up so that peaceable living and worship may be accomplished, the believer can still live in a quiet and peaceful way, not as to allow their lives or lifestyles to overshadow the Gospel at work within them.

NOTES ON TEXT

The passage makes mention of four different aspects of interaction with God: supplications, prayers, intercessions, and giving of thanks. This shows us that we are able to interact with God in different ways and interact on behalf of others in different ways. It is obvious that all are needed to establish flow in the Christian life, that believers may live peaceable and quietly with others, in harmony with both believer and non-believer alike. Intercession is an important – and vital – part of this.

POWER POINTS

- An intercessor is an individual who engages in intercession. As we can see from the word definitions earlier in this chapter, intercession is different from regular prayer in that it is defined as falling in with or meeting with. In the context of intercession, it is meeting with and falling in line with heaven for the sake of earthly petitions, and also meeting with the needs on earth and falling in line with things needed here. It is a literal state of wrangling with heaven on behalf of earth and, at the same time, wrangling with earth on behalf of heaven. The work of the intercessor is a vital function of this "in-between" job, realizing the ways that the natural and spiritual are deeply interconnected. It is a state of intervening in a deeper way to bring forth God's justice in the world (Isaiah 59:11-16).

- Intercession is mentioned along with petitions, prayers, intercession, and giving thanks because it is something that is done along with these other aspects. Many consider intercession a type of prayer, but the Bible does identify it as something else, a deeper positioning, if you will; it is an aspect of spiritual warfare by which the individual wrangles for the heavenly on earth and the earthly needs in heaven. Along with petitions, prayers, and giving thanks, intercession is to go forth for all people, everywhere, kings and those in authority, with the end goal that the church may live peaceably in the world. By doing this, it ensures that believers in the church will know how to conduct themselves rightly and powerfully, in each and every situation, and that the world will come to the full knowledge of Christ. By intercession as well as prayer in its various forms, we are able to be a witness to the world (I Timothy 2:1-7).

- The best Biblical example of an intercessor is that of Abraham, who interceded on behalf of Sodom and Gomorrah. When God announced He was going to destroy the cities, it was Abraham who stepped up and went before God in a "meeting" fashion. Recognizing God as just, Abraham was not challenging God; he was interceding and coming to a place where, recognizing both the heavenly and earthly positions, he petitioned God for the sake of the righteous, requesting that God show mercy on all for the sake of however many few there might have been. Wrangling with heaven for the sake of earth, Abraham learned that there was not even one individual who was righteous in the cities of Sodom and Gomorrah, but he still stood firm and spiritually fought for God's mercy and justice if righteous were present therein. (Genesis 18:16-33) Abraham's experience also reveals something important to us about intercession: it is not always successful, but that does not change the command to wrangle between heaven and earth, and stand in the gap for what is just and what is right.

- The Bible tells us that the best intercessor of all time is Jesus Christ (Isaiah 53:6-12, Hebrews 7:22-28). Not only is He our High Priest and the guarantor of a better covenant, He is also an intercessor. Jesus reveals to us the important role that intercessors play in salvation: that people are able to come to God because of the work of Christ. As intercessors participate in that work, they are able to spiritually battle and wrangle for the needs of people and the spiritual revelation that is so deeply needed as people come to a place of awareness and purpose.

- The struggles of Job remind us of how important having the right intercession is in our lives when we battle our own spiritual warfare. His friends, praying against him, were ineffective as intercessors on his behalf (Job 16:15-22). There are times when it is better for an intercessor not to pray, especially when they are wrangling against God's will in a way that will harm or deceive others (Jeremiah 7:15-20, Jeremiah 27:17-22). It is why the intercession of the Spirit is so vital for us as believers: because the Spirit does so within the complete will of God, working all things together for those of us who are called according to His purpose and who are being transformed from glory to glory and faith to faith (Romans 8:26-30).

- Many believe that intercession is exclusive to prophets, but the Bible does not state that intercession is a position reserved for prophets (Jeremiah 36:20-26). The Bible does state that prophets can serve in the function of an intercessor, and in many ways, it is compatible with the work of the prophet. In that vain, intercessors should be watching for the prophetic issues of the day, knowing how to intercede on behalf of God's righteousness, and trust that the remnant of grace shall be carried through as intercessors continue to wrangle between heaven and earth (Romans 11:1-5).

DIFFERENT WAYS INTERCESSION MAKES A DIFFERENCE

We should never assume that intercessors and the work of intercession does not make a difference spiritually or in people's lives. By looking at intercession from a Biblical perspective, we can see just how important intercession is, especially in the context of our lives in terms of salvation.

- **Addresses the seen and unseen** – A true intercessor doesn't always understand just what they are "wrangling" for or what it is all about. They may have a sense or an urge to go into the place of intercession to meet with heaven and strive for something or to go to an individual and strive for heaven, without fully understanding just what it is all about. Intercession helps to acknowledge and embrace that which we see and that which we don't see, recognizing the connection spoken of earlier between the spiritual and the natural.

- **Connect the Body in unity through spiritual warfare** – We don't often think of spiritual warfare as a source of unity, but it is. The reasons we have so many problems in church today often stem from the fact that while we might know how to pray against things, we don't know how to stand corporately as a church, ready for battle, doing the work that Jesus has commissioned us to do as a Kingdom. The intercessor's work reminds us that spiritual warfare is more than just yelling at the devil, and that contenting in prayer for people requires more than just prayer: it also requires action.

- **A heavenly and an earthly perspective** – The intercessor's perspective is both heavenly and earthly, which gives all of us who are here on earth a greater understanding of the heavenly and the spiritual realm. Avoiding the temptation to get so holy that we are no earthly good comes about as we understand the balance that the intercessor can teach all of us so we can be better witnesses for the Lord, right where we are.

INTERCESSORS IN HISTORY

We know that many people in history have prayed, and finding people who were specifically known for their intercession has been a challenge...but I was able to find a few who we can trust sat in the function of intercessor at some point in their lives.

- **Gertrude of Helfta (1256-1302)** – Even though we know little about the life of Gertrude of Helfta, her written works and the depth of which she loved God and sought to pray and intercede for the benefits of the world. She spent most of her life in a monastery, including her education from age four. She joined the monastic community herself in 1266, and her strong education shines through in her great works. Gertrude experienced a series of visions throughout her life, that changed her life's priorities away from earthly things and focused more on the spiritual, especially prayer, meditation, and intercession. She was of great renown in the seventeenth-century, especially in

France, because of the piety and spiritual perspective found in her writings.[17]

- **Andrew Murray (1828-1917)** – The written works of Andrew Murray, particularly on the work of prayer and intercession, are some of the most classic Christian writings in history. His words on these essential topics reveal to us the heart of a man who truly understood what intercession and prayer were both about. The son of a Dutch Reformed Church missionary in South Africa, Andrew Murray received the best theological education available in Europe and, in the process, became a member of the Het Reveil, a religious revival spreading through the Netherlands at the time. He worked in different missions and spent his life staunchly believing in the continuation of the apostolic gifts and in faith healing. He is, therefore, a significant ancestor of the Pentecostal Movement.[18]

- **Corrie Ten Boom (1892-1983)** – You probably noticed that we started the chapter with a quote by Corrie Ten Boom about intercession, and now we are going to see how her important intercession impacted the lives of individuals in her generation. Born in Amsterdam, the Netherlands, Corrie Ten Boom was a watchmaker, the leader of a church for people with mental disabilities, and a foster parent when the Nazis invaded the Netherlands in 1940. Directly confronted with Nazi authority (they shut down one of her charitable organizations), Corrie Ten Boom was moved to help the work of the Jews and others who resisted the Nazi invasion in the Netherlands, all of whom were persecuted by the Nazis during World War II. She began the "Hiding Place," using her own house as a place of refuge for these people. It has been said that she may very well have saved hundreds of people as she interceded between heaven and earth, literally standing in warfare, just by doing the right thing.[19]

- **Watchman Nee (1903-1972)** – Most Christians who are familiar with modern church history (especially in the context of international church movements) have heard of Watchman Nee and the incredible work he did to develop the church in China. What many do not know is in a few of his works, Watchman Nee revealed much about the intercessory role and the need for intercession in the church. Born in China as the third of nine children, Watchman Nee was born Ni Tuoseng in 1903. He was baptized into the Methodist Church as an infant. As a result of revival meetings, Watchman Nee was profoundly moved to become a Christian for himself and put aside anything that might hinder his call. He trained to be in ministry and was influenced on many different strains of Christian traditions, and became a prolific pastor and writer throughout his years. He was imprisoned after the Communist Revolution and spent his last twenty years of life in prison.[20]

QUESTIONS AND ANSWERS

- **What is intercessory prayer?**

  Many people assume that intercessory prayer is the same type of work as intercession, but this assumption is incorrect. Intercessory prayer is simply a type of prayer that requests on behalf of another or on behalf of a situation. It is frequently done before church services or special events in order to set the proper atmosphere for what is to come. There is nothing wrong with intercessory prayer, but one should understand that just because they engage in intercessory prayer, that does not make them an intercessor.

- **Does an intercessor need to be licensed and ordained?**

The work of the intercessor itself does not require a license nor an ordination. If one is an intercessor as a function of a five-fold ministry office or an appointment, license and ordination are in order.

- **Are there different types of intercessors?**

While some might disagree with me (and a search on the internet would confirm their disagreement), the Bible doesn't give orders or delegate types of intercessors. In fact, aside from the verses we discussed earlier in the Bible, there aren't any other verses that discuss intercession or intercessors. Often what people do who try to assign different types to intercession is assume certain Biblical characters were intercessors, which is speculative. They also attribute characteristics to intercession that are not characteristic of a true intercessor. While someone's spiritual or five-fold gifts may impact the way they intercede or may affect exactly how they do their intercessory work, the work of an intercessor is still foundationally the same.

- **Should ministries have teams of intercessors?**

I have heard a lot of arguments, both ways, about intercessors in ministry. One extreme I heard of recently was a person who felt each minister needed at least twenty intercessors, constantly interceding for that ministry. I have also heard of people who believe that leaders don't need them. The answer to me is somewhere in the middle. I think having people to intercede for a ministry is a powerful and important thing, but let's also never nullify the job of every person who is covered by or somehow a part of a ministry to pray for that ministry work. Yes, intercession is important, but it is not the only thing, nor the most important thing. I don't know if ministries need mass teams of intercessors, but they do need at least one or two solid, proven intercessors to help guide those who pray for the ministry and help contend for the spiritual warfare that goes on therein.

- **Can intercessors manifest physical symptoms of their spiritual battles?**

It depends on the intercessor. Physical manifestations of spiritual things goes more under the heading of being a mystic than an intercessor (and we will talk about mystics later in this book), but I have heard of some intercessors who do experience physical discomforts as a part of their spiritual alerts, letting them know what to intercede about or to pay attention to certain matters in the spiritual realm (and they were not individuals who were mystics). I would say It Is entirely possible, but most likely, a rare aspect of intercession.

- **Should an intercessor be trained?**

As with all things spiritual, I believe intercessors should be trained by either apostles or prophets (or ideally, both) in the different aspects of the supernatural and in different issues that pertain to spiritual warfare, different types of prayer, and different aspects of spiritual discernment. This is something that can, and should, be offered through ministries and churches.

DISCUSSION, STUDY AND REVIEW QUESTIONS

1. Have people always been known to pray for themselves? How does the Apostle Paul advise people pray? Why was this method of prayer important for the church?

2. What are four different methods for interaction with God? What does this show us? Are all necessary for the flow in

the Christian life? Why or why not? What should believers aim for? What role does intercession play in all of this?

3. What is an intercessor? How is intercession different from prayer? What is intercession? How does the work of the intercessor reveal that heaven and earth are connected?

4. Why is intercession mentioned along with forms of prayer? Is intercession a form of prayer? Why or why not? What is it? How does intercession help the believers to live peaceably and as a right witness in the world?

5. Who is the best Biblical example of an intercessor? What did this individual do, and why was it important? What does it teach us about intercession and the nature of the work? Do the visible results of intercession change the work any? Why or why not?

6. Who was the best intercessor of all time? In addition to an intercessor, what else is Jesus in our lives? What does Jesus reveal to us about intercessors?

7. What does Job's experience reveal to us about intercession and intercessors? Are there times when it is better for an intercessor not to pray? Why or why not? Why is the intercession of the Spirit so vital for us as believers?

8. Is intercession exclusive to prophets? Why or why not? Can prophets operate as intercessors? What do intercessors need to pay attention to as part of their function?

9. What are some different ways that intercession makes a difference?

10. Who were some notable intercessors in history?

11. Discuss and share some of the questions and answers found in the "Questions and Answers" section. What did you learn that you did not know about intercessors and intercession? What did you learn that changed your mind about an opinion you might have had prior about intercessors and intercession? How did learning about specific issues related to intercessors and intercession help you to grow in your understanding of intercessors and intercession? The church? Your own relationship with God?

12. Who is your favorite intercessor? Why are they your favorite?

Seven ● WATCHMAN AND GATEKEEPER

When Luther made his statement, it was placed on the church door, or church gate. This initiated the Reformation. As gatekeeper and watchman of my home, I guard its gates carefully as well as those of my church and city.
– Carl Townsend[1]

A topic often raised whenever a disaster of some sort happens, the work of the watchman and gatekeeper are often assigned to prophets and disregarded for others (we will discuss that issue more later). It's quite obvious, however, that whoever is assigned to these functions is clearly falling down on the job. With the number of different attacks on the church, the various spiritual invasions that seem to occur with regularity in ministries all over the world, and the intense exhaustion, lack of spiritual discipline, and lack of interest within ministries themselves, many different spiritual presences have invaded the church because those who are assigned to watch out and guard the church have gone off duty.

Like the dreamer and visionary, the watchman and gatekeeper have been mentioned here because their roles are very similar: to note things and keep them out. We know that there have been many shifts in the church and in ways that things are perceived spiritually, and the issue of the gatekeeper and watchman are no different. As many people are eager to preach and be noticed rather than stand and watch, we are keenly aware that new gatekeepers and watchmen must be assigned, ready and prepared to observe and keep track of the movements of the church and be ready to sound the word of protection when the enemy comes in like a flood.

TEXT STUDY

2 Samuel 18:24-33

POWER TEXTS

2 Kings 7:3-12, I Chronicles 9:17-34, 2 Chronicles 23:18-21, Psalm 127:1-2, Job 27:13-23, Nehemiah 7:1-73, Nehemiah 10:37-39, Isaiah 21:1-12, Ezekiel 3:16-21, Ezekiel 33:1-20, Hosea 9:7-9, John 10:1-18.

POWER VERSE

2 Samuel 18:26:

- *"And the watchman saw another man running: and the watchman called unto the porter, and said, Behold another man running alone. And the king said, He also bringeth tidings."*

- *"Then the watchman saw another man running, and he called down to the gatekeeper, 'Look, another man running alone!.' The king said, 'He must be bringing good news, too.'"* (NIV)

- *"The watchman saw another man running toward them. He shouted down, 'Here comes another one.' And the king replied, 'He will have more news.'"* (TLB)

- *"The watchman saw another man running toward them.*

He shouted down, 'Here comes another one!' The king replied, 'He also will have news.' (NLT)

- *"The espyer saw another man running; and the espyer cried on high, and said, Another man running alone appeareth to me. And the king said to him, And this man is a good messenger."* (WYC)

- *"When the watchman saw another man running, the watchman called, 'There's another man running alone.' The king said, 'This one is also bringing good news.'"* (GW)

POWER WORDS

- **Watchman** – From the Hebrew word *tsaphah* which means, "to look out or about, spy, keep watch, observe, watch."[2]

- **Running** – From the Hebrew word *ruwts* which means "to run."[3]

- **Called** – From the Hebrew word *qara'* which means "to call, call out, recite, read, cry out, proclaim."[4]

- **Porter** – From the Hebrew word *show`er* which means, "gatekeeper, porter."[5]

- **Bringeth tidings** – From the Hebrew word *basar*, which means, "to bear news, bear tidings, publish, preach, show forth."[6]

HISTORICAL CONTEXT

In the ancient world, watchmen and gatekeepers were the "alarm systems" of their day. Watchmen did exactly what it sounds like they did: they stood on the watch, kind of like a security guard, and monitored the perimeter of a castle, fortress, or city, watching and monitoring as far as they were able to see. They would sit high up and watch over the wall of an area, monitoring for foreign invaders. Gatekeepers had the job of monitoring a gate or door, making sure that not just anyone could enter into a building or location freely. Both the watchman and the gatekeeper kept borders and perimeters tight and structured, protected and guarded against invaders, and made sure that the established order remained established, even in the face of invading forces.

NOTES ON TEXT

In our central text, we are able to see how watchmen and gatekeepers (referred to as porters in the King James Version) worked together to monitor visitors and forces. The watchman took note of who approached and the gatekeeper was prepared for whatever came to enter the gate. Spiritual watchmen and gatekeepers are a part of the same work: protection and defense, monitoring and being aware of what is going on to guard the church.

POWER POINTS

- The watchman and the gatekeeper provide a dual defense to monitor and prepare for that which is seeking to approach or invade a place. The two work together: with the watchman on alert around the perimeter and the gatekeeper on alert at the door or gate. By observing movements and operations, the watchman and gatekeeper are able to assess what is coming and whether or not it is fit to enter (2 Samuel 18:24-33).

- The work of watchmen and gatekeepers was both sacred and secular in ancient times. This tells us that spiritual watchmen and gatekeepers have the responsibility to monitor the movement of different things that may be in their atmosphere, in order to maintain the spiritual status quo of a given situation (2 Kings 7:3-12, Nehemiah 7:1-73).

- Watchmen are guardians as well as monitors. The watchman operates over the church or ministry he or she is a part of, over the house that the Lord has built, over their own immediate house and over households in general, over cities, nations, and regions. They are individuals who are constantly on duty: having to awake early or stay up late, in order to make sure that the spiritual watches are met. During these watches, a watchman may pray, praise God, or monitor different spiritual activities, awaiting word from God about how to respond (Psalm 127:1-2). They are positioned in a certain place (commonly called a watchtower in ancient times) and ready to stand at their post, monitoring the night, monitoring when dawn comes, and monitoring each and every change that shifts as things come and go (Isaiah 21:1-12). Spiritual watchmen must position themselves to be able to see and prepare themselves to be able to move and call out for warnings as necessary.

- Watchmen are a powerful warning and alert signal, notifying about impurities or imperfections within a place. Watchmen also identify and see sin and different impurities that may attempt to come into a church, a ministry, or an individual's life, and they seek to warn about them (Ezekiel 3:16-21). God appoints an individual for the function of a watchman, and even if the people do not hear the warning of the watchman, the watchman still must herald the important message (Ezekiel 33:1-19). The watchman reminds us that what we do is seen and heard by God, and that we cannot fool Him. Even if others feel our deeds are righteous or we pretend to be notable for what we are doing in the sight of others, the watchman proves that God sees and knows all, even our innermost motives (Job 27:13-23).

- Gatekeepers are specifically mentioned as part of the temple work in the Old Testament. These were individuals who made sure they were stationed and positioned to protect the gate, particularly the gate that was a part of the Levite camp (1 Chronicles 9:17-34). We learn that they all had specific duties as part of gatekeeping: monitoring articles used in temple service, care for furnishings and other articles, Sabbath preparation, items used in sacrifices, the rooms and treasuries of the ministry, and they were in charge of monitoring the temple at night and being the ones who opened it in the morning. More than just being individuals who watched a door, they were responsible for the security of the temple. The gatekeepers today have a similar duty: they are responsible to be stationed and positioned to protect the church, protect the church buildings, protect the church's valuables, and protect the leadership in the church. Gatekeepers represent a guardianship position, essential for proper ministry function. Through the work of the gatekeeper, nothing unclean or improper can enter the church from a spiritual perspective (2 Chronicles 23:18-21).

- Thanks to the gatekeepers, the house of God is never neglected. The items brought in to the storehouse for the benefit of the ministry and the continued survival of ministers is monitored in the locations where the gatekeepers' items are also kept (Nehemiah 10:37-39). This shows gatekeepers to be trusted and important people, reliable in every way.

- Many assume the role of watchman and gatekeeper to be assigned to prophets, but the Bible does not support this exclusivity. The role of the watchman and the gatekeeper were secular positions, not strictly spiritual, and individuals held these roles in a secular role were not prophets. What the Bible does state, however, is that prophets should be alert and should be acting as watchmen (Hosea 9:7-9) and that leaders should take on the responsibility of being spiritual gatekeepers (John 10:1-18). This does not mean it is their responsibility alone, however; leaders need the essential help of those who function in these offices to alert and warn, as we can see in the role of watchmen and gatekeepers in the Bible.

WAYS TO ENGAGE WATCHMEN AND GATEKEEPERS INTO A MINISTRY

The work of watchmen and gatekeepers, as we can see, is both spiritual and practical. Many people think, however, that taking on these works is akin to taking on a full-blown ministry office. This does not have to be the case, and those who are interested in works related to gatekeeping and watchmen should be encouraged to participate in activities that relate to their functional service.

- **Pray for the ministry and the needs of the community** – Watchmen and gatekeepers don't just observe things, they take action to prevent oncoming issues or disasters. Churches, ministries, leaders, and communities need the prayers of the faithful in order to sustain and encourage them through difficult and good times. Organize prayer watches, have special events, incorporate different trainings, and encourage people to get involved!

- **Get involved in church or ministry security** – A practical aspect to gatekeeping and watchmen is to care about the actual physical structure of a church or ministry. Today ministers spend thousands of dollars to have bodyguards and personal protective security, which is a severe drain on ministries financially. The issue of ministry and church security can be solved by instituting gatekeepers and watchmen to care for the valuables, the buildings, the property, and the leaders of the church, rather than having to rely on outside forces to implement safety.

- **Participate in church or ministry in a new way** – The work of a watchman and a gatekeeper is relatively straightforward, but there are many ways these works can be integrated into a church or ministry. Someone who operates in one or both of these functions can easily serve in other aspects of ministry service, however they are gifted. Get involved and see ways that spiritual insight and perceptiveness can benefit a ministry work in a larger way.

WATCHMEN AND GATEKEEPERS IN HISTORY

Very few individuals in history have identified themselves as "watchmen" or "gatekeepers" in a spiritual sense. That doesn't mean, however, that they did not perform the work of these vital functions. Here are some individuals who, through their lives and their dedication, functioned as watchmen and gatekeepers.

- **Alexander Akimetes (d. 403)** – Recognizing the importance of continual prayer day and night, Alexander Akimetes was a hermit and founder of religious centers after his conversion to Christianity. After spending eleven years as a hermit, he realized the importance of work in establishing communities and doing mission work. It was his vision to hold prayer service in which four hundred monks chanted the Divine Office throughout the day and night, twenty-four hours per day.[7]

- **Leboa (710-782)** – Leboa (also spelled Lioba and Leofgyth) was an Anglo-Saxon woman who became a nun and a missionary to the Germans. She was born into nobility and her birth itself was considered to be a miracle by the family. After having a dream that represented the leadership she was to have in her life, she spent her life in service through prayer, education, teaching, and counsel. It was believed that she was able to halt a storm at her very command, and was the only woman allowed to enter into male monasteries for church scholarship and consultation. She evangelized cities, considered a friend of politicians, and was credited with working many miracles (including protecting the reputation of the nuns in her care and performing healings).[8]

- **Olga of Kiev (890-969)** – We don't know much about Olga of Kiev's early life, but we do know that she played a very important role as a literal spiritual watchman and gatekeeper in a governmental position. She worked as a government regent over Kievan Rus. When people came and tried to persuade her to marry a foreign people and forsake her rule, she took quick action to see that her enemies were killed. She was the first ruler of this region to convert to Christianity and clearly saw her duty to protect the integrity of the nation therein.[9]

- **Rees Howells (1879-1950)** – Rees Howells was the founder of the Bible College of Wales. He was a man who believed in the power of prayer and, recognizing the importance of keeping spiritual watch and intercession alike, began twenty-four hour prayer sessions to pray for the nations. He and his wife were later missionaries to Africa, and it was his watchful spirit that kept intercession going long enough to see revival break out across southern Africa between 1915 and 1920.[10]

QUESTIONS AND ANSWERS

- **What are the eight watches of the day and night?**

Prayer watches are three-hour blocks of time scattered throughout the day in which certain prayers and intercessions are to be made during those hours. Many individuals interested in being spiritual watchmen pray according to the eight watches, which are:

- o First watch – 6 PM – 9 PM
- o Second watch – 9 PM – 12 AM
- o Third watch – 12 AM – 3 AM
- o Fourth watch – 3 AM – 6 AM
- o Fifth watch – 6 AM – 9 AM
- o Sixth watch – 9 AM – 12 PM
- o Seventh watch – 12 PM – 3 PM
- o Eighth watch – 3 PM – 6 PM

Different belief systems advocate different types of prayer during these hours and encourage the person who prays with the eight watches to be alert to pray for specific spiritual and demonic activity that rises during those times.

- **What relationship do gatekeeping and watchmen have to intercessors?**

It is obvious from this chapter that gatekeepers and watchmen work together. Intercessors should also be working with gatekeepers and watchmen, because their work can alert the intercessor to spiritual battle. In essence, all of the functions should work together, alerting the others who function in these works to tasks and issues that need attention.

- **Should husbands and wives be watchmen and gatekeepers over their homes?**

Anyone who has a home or an apartment or lives somewhere with a leadership position should position themselves as watchmen and gatekeepers over their domiciles. This relates spiritually, through materials that come into the home, through people who come into the home, and as well through guarding the priorities and attitudes that people have within that home. It is a balancing act of respect, of love, of principle, and of respect. In every home, love should be guarded and things that attempt to destroy that should be monitored.

- **Can women be watchmen and gatekeepers?**

The role of a spiritual watchman and gatekeeper is not gender-specific, and women as well as men can perform these functions.

- **Do watchmen and gatekeepers do their work full-time?**

The functions of a watchman or gatekeeper are not a full-time ministry work, but one that is shared among other individuals and done as a part of an existing work or ministry. They are not independent of themselves, nor do they require full-time status.

- **Should watchmen and gatekeepers receive training?**

In the same vain as I had mentioned with intercessors, watchmen and gatekeepers should be trained by their covering ministries, for the needs and purposes that exist within the ministries where they are. Watchmen and gatekeepers do not exist independently of another ministry. The training does not need to be as comprehensive as minister's training, but should relate to information and things that will help that watchman or gatekeeper excel in spiritual observations, prayer, ministry assistance and security, and excel in their functions. They should be educated in different aspects of spiritual warfare, prayer, helps ministry, in Scripture studies and exegesis, in Bible history and culture, and in church history, among any other area of education that a church can think of that will help a watchman or gatekeeper keep the borders of the ministry in effective working order.

DISCUSSION, STUDY AND REVIEW QUESTIONS

1. In ancient times, what purpose did gatekeepers and watchmen provide? What did watchmen do? How did they position themselves for their work? What did gatekeepers do? What did the two works do in order to guard perimeters and properties?

2. How did watchmen and gatekeepers work together? Are they a part of the same work?

3. What dual defense do watchmen and gatekeepers work together? What assessment are watchmen and gatekeepers equipped to make?

4. Was the work of the watchman and gatekeeper secular as well as sacred? What does this tell us about them from a spiritual perspective?

5. What two things are watchmen? What do watchmen watch over? What are some of the things a watchman must do to keep watch over their territory? What do watchmen do during their watches? How did watchmen of old position themselves? How should spiritual watchmen of today position themselves?

6. What kind of alert do watchmen provide? What do watchmen see and notify about? Should a watchman alert about their message even if it is not accepted? Why or why not? What does the watchman remind us about?

7. What specific work were gatekeepers a part of in the Old Testament? What were some of the specific duties of

gatekeepers? What are some specific duties of gatekeepers today?

8. Do the gatekeepers make sure that the house of God has no lack? How do they do this? What kind of people should gatekeepers be?

9. Are watchmen and gatekeepers only prophets? What connections exist between the watchmen, gatekeepers, prophets and leaders?

10. What are some ways we can engage watchmen and gatekeepers in a ministry?

11. Who were some notable watchmen and gatekeepers in history?

12. Discuss and share some of the questions and answers found in the "Questions and Answers" section. What did you learn that you did not know about watchmen and gatekeepers? What did you learn that changed your mind about an opinion you might have had prior about watchmen and gatekeepers? How did learning about specific issues related to watchmen and gatekeepers help you to grow in your understanding of watchmen and gatekeepers? The church? Your own relationship with God?

13. Who is your favorite watchman or gatekeeper? Why are they your favorite?

Eight ● HANDMAIDEN AND MALE SERVANT

You are what you do, not what you say you'll do.
– Carl Gustav Jung[1]

W E all know that Christians are called to service, but we do not recognize that being in service is an important function of the church. If believers are not in service, then the church is unable to move forward in its proclamation of the Gospel. Even though we emphasize being served today, we have forgotten the essential and important role that merits being of service. Jesus calls those who follow Him to make themselves the servants of all, especially those that we deem the "least of these." This means that Christians of every situation, denomination, belief system, serve the world because Jesus has called them to do so.

For this reason, it is important that we talk about the function of handmaidens and male servants. Many have started organizations with these titles or proclaim themselves to be these things without understanding what they are saying, and as a result, they misrepresent what they are to others. Handmaidens and male servants are just that – servants – albeit they are a specific type of servant which relates to the work that they do in both the world and in the Kingdom.

TEXT STUDY

Acts 2:14-21

POWER TEXTS

Genesis 16:1-16, Exodus 21:1-36, Ruth 2:10-14, 1 Samuel 1:4-18, 2 Kings 4:1-17, Psalm 86:12-17, Psalm 119:5-16, Isaiah 14:1-5, Jeremiah 34:10-16, Luke 1:35-55, Luke 12:34-47.

POWER VERSE

Acts 2:18:

- *"And on My servants and on My handmaidens I will pour out in those days of My Spirit; and they shall prophesy."*

- *"Yea, even upon My bondmen and upon My bondwomen in those days will I pour out of My Spirit, and they shall prophesy."* (DARBY)

- *"At that time I will pour out My Spirit also on My male slaves [servants] and female slaves [servants], and they will prophesy."* (EXB)

- *"Even on My servants, both men and women, I will pour out My Spirit in those days, and they will prophesy."* (NET)

- *"Yes, in those days I shall offer My Spirit to all servants, both male and female, and they will boldly speak My word."* (VOICE)

- *"Yes, and on My menservants also and on my maidservants in those days I will pour out of My Spirit, and they shall prophesy [telling forth the divine counsels and predicting future events pertaining especially to God's Kingdom]."* (AMP)

POWER WORDS

- **Servants** – From the Greek word *doulos* which means, "a slave, bondman, man of servile condition; a servant, attendant."[2]

- **Handmaidens** – From the Greek word *doule* which means "a female slave, bondmaid, handmaid."[3]

- **Pour out** – From the Greek word *ekcheo* which means "to pour out, shed forth; metaph. to bestow or distribute largely."[4]

- **Days** – From the Greek word *hemera* which means "the day, used of the natural day, or the interval between sunrise and sunset, as distinguished from and contrasted with the night; of the civil day, or the space of twenty four hours (thus including the night); of the last day of this present age, the day Christ will return from heaven, raise the dead, hold the final judgment, and perfect His kingdom; used of time in general, i.e. the days of his life.[5]

- **Spirit** – From the Greek word *pneuma,* which means "a movement of air (a gentle blast); the spirit, i.e. the vital principal by which the body is animated; a spirit, i.e. a simple essence, devoid of all or at least all grosser matter, and possessed of the power of knowing, desiring, deciding, and acting; of God; the disposition or influence which fills and governs the soul of any one."[6]

- **Prophecy** – From the Greek word *propheteuo* which means, "to prophesy, to be a prophet, speak forth by divine inspirations, to predict, to prophesy, with the idea of foretelling future events pertaining esp. to the kingdom of

God, to utter forth, declare, a thing which can only be known by divine revelation, to break forth under sudden impulse in lofty discourse or praise of the divine counsels, under like prompting, to teach, refute, reprove, admonish, comfort others, to act as a prophet, discharge the prophetic office."[7]

HISTORICAL CONTEXT

Under the law of the Old Testament, prophecy was limited to the handful of men and women who served as prophets and prophetesses. Service of the Lord was left to the Levites, who served as priests in the temple. Speaking for God was a rarity, and very few people were given the opportunity to do so. The outpouring of the Spirit on the feast of Pentecost (still available to the believer today) empowers Christians to serve God and to know His Spirit and His voice in their lives as they go forth as His servants, both male and female servants.

NOTES ON TEXT

It is very important that we fully see that God has called us His sons and daughters, His old and His young, and His servants and handmaidens, with no contradiction between the six categories. We are the sons and daughters of God who, whether young are old, are also given the privilege to serve as His menservants and maidservants. In addition to seeing visions, dreaming dreams, and seeing many signs and wonders in the heavens and the earth, we will also be able to prophesy. As believers, it is essential we see ourselves as a part of this work and process, because we are not just called to be sons and daughters, or young and old, but servants who are personally invested in the assignment, work, and welfare of the One Who we serve.

POWER POINTS

- In the context of Acts 2:18, the prophecy was speaking of two specific types of servant, and these were menservants or handmaidens (Acts 2:14-21). They were so-called because they were literally 'at hand' at any time (within the realm of their master) as needed. The work of the men's servant and handmaiden were as personal attendants to their master, men and women who did shopping, dressing, and ran errands for the man or woman of the house, and travelled with them, as well. They made sure that, at all times, the man and woman of the house were to be satisfied, well-cared for, and most of all, well-represented. The work of the menservant and handmaiden was to ensure that the man or woman of the house had the proper image and was properly taken care of. The Bible clarifies that, endowed with His Spirit, we are not just servants of everybody or of a household, but of the Almighty God, endowed with the ability to represent Him well and do His work in the earth. As God has promised that those servants who are oppressed would one day rule (Isaiah 14:1-5), we can know that our servanthood for God will render us rulership in His Kingdom after Jesus returns.

- The law of slaves applied to handmaidens and to menservants (Exodus 21:1-36). They were considered the property of their owners, and were to serve for mandated periods of time (Jeremiah 34:10-16). In the case of many handmaidens and menservants, they stayed and worked with their masters for life, out of a sense of love and service. This meant their work as servants was a choice, and that they became servants for life. Many in the Bible recognized their role as a life-long servant of God, and also heralded the fact that their mothers were also life-long handmaidens of the Lord, as part of their commitment to Him (Psalm 86:12-17, Psalm 119:5-16).

- Menservants and handmaidens were willing to do anything they were asked by their masters, even things we might consider extreme or outlandish by modern standards (Genesis 16:1-16). The menservant and handmaiden had a different quality about them, an excellent one, that was fully willing and ready for any sort of circumstance, moment, or situation that would cause their master to call. They were known for having a spirit of excellence (Ruth 2:10-14).

- A true handmaiden and menservant will be ready and prepared, at all times, for whatever is needed. They look for each and every opportunity to serve and do so with a good understanding and a good attitude. Even though the master may take longer than expected, they are ready and watching, waiting to go forth. Spiritual handmaidens and menservants are ready and waiting for God's command to come forth so they can serve Him with excellence in all that they day. They know that as part of their work they must be obedient and never know just where God will have them to be or do next. While they await new orders, they continue in obedience for the orders they already have (Luke 12:34-47).

- The power of servanthood is displayed powerfully in the widow woman and the Shunammite woman. Both had impossible situations but both still knew they were handmaids, or personal servants, of God. When we are His handmaidens and His menservants, all things are possible, because He takes care of His servants (2 Kings 4:1-17).

- Mary, mother of Jesus, and Hannah, mother of Samuel, both referred to themselves as "handmaidens" of the Lord (1 Samuel 1:4-18, Luke 1:35-55). They knew and recognized the powerful way that God had moved throughout history, and knew that they desired to be His servants, no matter how difficult the tasks associated with that would be. Both show us the power of servanthood and the way that entrusting our lives as God's servants (both men and women) helps to see the impact we can make on humanity down through the generations.

ATTITUDES OF MENSERVANTS AND HANDMAIDENS

It's not a big secret that attitude is an issue when we deal with today's church. People think they are above training and often assume titles and offices they are unprepared to receive. Before any one of us receives an office, an appointment, a spiritual gift, a title, or whatever you want to call it, every single one of us should first know and how to function as servants of the Lord, as individuals who receive their commands from God rather than the advice or ideas of others.

- **Know how to follow** – We've heard It said that good leaders make good followers, and this is very true. People who do not understand guidance from others who are led by God do not understand how to be directly led by God Himself. We can never assume that God is just a big version of us, and that every idea or thought we have is from God. We learn this from our dedication to our own ministry leaders, being willing to serve and assist, as necessary, whether ordained or not.

- **Know how to give** – Being the servant of God is about giving of one's entire life, however God desires to use it. We get very defiant when we start talking about things being our lives or being our material goods, but when we decide that we are going to be the servants of God, we are required to give of our whole selves, and specifically that which He asks us to give. As much as we don't like to admit it, nothing is off the table with God, and some of what He asks might be hard or difficult. I will say, however, that it's a lot harder to accept when we don't already have training in giving, and we are stingy with what we are willing to part with. True handmaidens and menservants are willing to give, anything and everything, as God instructs.

- **Know they don't do the work of God alone** – Ancient domestic systems were complex, involving many different members of a household staff (both men and women) in order to keep the house running, meals cooked, clothes clean, and personal needs met of the household members. The domestics of a household knew that they could not get the jobs done by themselves, especially the bigger the house. Even houses with one or two staff members were very dependent upon good systems and outside help to keep up with matters. A true handmaiden and menservant knows that there are other servants of God working, whether they know them or not, and know better than to scorn or forsake others who are getting the same jobs done, just in different ways.

HANDMAIDENS AND MENSERVANTS IN HISTORY

We know that in the past two thousand years, there have been a countless number of people who have served as handmaidens and menservants of the Lord. Here, even though we have limited space to share only a few, we pay tribute to these fine servants of God throughout the ages.

- **Philip Romolo Neri (1515-1595)** – Called "the Apostle of Rome," Philip Neri started a secular clergy order known as the Congregation of the Oratory. He was born into nobility and received the best education available from a Dominican monastery in Florence. For a few years, he worked as a tutor and expanded his own education through personal study. He then started working among the poor and prostitutes of the city, actively evangelizing all who would listen. He became a priest and considered becoming a missionary, but was dissuaded with the amount of work to do in Rome. He set up his event structure to involve singing of hymns, prayers, and readings of Scripture, done throughout the city at different churches (which was unheard of at the time). As a result of his efforts, he gained many converts, and had many people desiring to become a part of his work too, which led to the foundation of the Congregation of the Oratory, which also came with the founding of his own parish church. His wonderful countenance that was in stark contrast with the clergy of his day that were disinterested and uncaring showed that being a servant of God is much more than just wearing a robe and a title.[8]

- **Titus Coan (1801-1881)** – Titus Coan was an American Christian missionary who lived much of his life working in Gospel proclamation on the Hawaiian Islands. Despite the loss of his first wife and all four of his children, he still heard God's call to learn the Hawaiian language and educate the people on the islands about the Lord. Known as the "Bishop of Kilauea," he directed the construction of Haili Church and also later did an extensive speaking tour throughout the United States. For many years, he also observed the move of volcanoes and sent observations relating to volcanic eruptions to a geologist. He was valued by both the Christian and scientific communities of his time.[9]

- **Evangeline Cory Booth (1865-1950)** – The daughter of William and Catherine Booth, Evangeline became the fourth general of the Salvation Army and was also its first female General. She spent many years, starting at age 15, selling The War Cry newspaper in London and a corps officer by age 21. She worked as a Field Commissioner in Great Britain and worked among the poorest of the poor, rowdy crowds, and later as Territorial Commander of the United States and Canada. Despite a family dispute, Evangeline became the fourth leader of the Salvation Army in 1934. The organization prospered and expanded under her leadership, including the spread of the organization into seven new countries. Surely her lifetime of dedication as a handmaiden of the Lord speaks volumes to all of us who follow unto this day![10]

- **Dr. Ida Sophia Scudder (1870-1960)** – Dr. Ida Scudder started out her life as daughter to medical missionaries, particularly in India. Throughout her childhood, she watched the plight of the Indian people. Even though she expected to get married and settle into a normal life after studying at Northfield Seminary, God had another plan for her. When visiting her mother in India, she witnessed the travesty of women who died in childbirth without cause due to poor medical care. She believed God spoke to her through this experience, and dedicated her life to missions (including remaining single for her work). She was a part of the first class that accepted women at Cornell Medical College and then returned to India to start her work. With a grant, she started a small dispensary and clinic for women at Vellore. In two years, she treated five thousand patients. Realizing the need for reinforcements, she opened a medical school for girls, with over one hundred and fifty applicants in the first year. She is credited with starting one of Asia's most important teaching hospitals which remains today, the Christian Medical College and Hospital.[11]

QUESTIONS AND ANSWERS

- **Why is service a part of the Gospel process?**

We can see in the Gospels how difficult it was to get things done when people were so obviously fighting for position rather than focusing on spiritual service. Jesus Himself even reprimanded the first disciples for trying to outdo each other, arguing over who was the greatest. Human nature is competitive, and it demands that we submit ourselves to

God's order in order to accomplish His work. Knowing that we are called to serve is essential to make sure that we know what is right, teach what is right, and do exactly what God has called us to do as we exercise His will in our lives rather than our own.

- **Does being a handmaiden and menservant of the Lord demand that we serve one another?**

Since that is what Jesus commanded us to do, that is precisely one of the ways we are in obedience to His will. It is a primary way we serve God, by serving others.

- **Many use the term "handmaiden" or "menservant" to indicate someone is single. Is this a rule?**

Servants of men all throughout history have been both married and single. The same is true for the servants of God. There were many people in history who remained single to focus exclusively on spiritual work, and there are others who focused on spiritual work with their spouse and their families in tow. Whether single or married, the call to be a servant of God does not change. It just means that when someone does decide to marry, they must make sure their spouse is on the same page with their desire to serve the Lord completely and without question.

- **How old should handmaidens and menservants be?**

A handmaiden and menservant must understand the commitment and choice they are making to serve God. That means that a handmaiden or menservant makes this decision to function for God in this way when they are ready to do so, at the point in their lives when God becomes real and they are aware of service.

- **Where do I start as a menservant or handmaiden?**

  Instead of seeing these as foreign, outlandish things that can never be accomplished by an ordinary person, embrace the concept of being a servant as a part of everyday life. We should be doing good things, because these things make our faith real to others. We should help out our neighbors and volunteer on different projects and help out at church. We should learn how we can be better members in our families and how to be better people. Study the history of the faith and learn all the different ways people have served God. Be an individual who is involved and active in loving and working with other people.

- **How do I recognize the voice of God unto obedience in my life?**

  We often think of the voice of God as something distant and leading down a hallway that brings us to an enlightened door of opportunity. The reality about hearing from God is far different than that. God can speak to us through a situation; through a need that exists; through a circumstance; or through someone else, especially our leadership. We will often get confirmation of what God wants us to do, and the ways God wants us to serve. As we go through life, we must pay attention to the senses that we have, the way God moves through us, and through the things that most need doing all around us.

DISCUSSION, STUDY AND REVIEW QUESTIONS

1. Who was limited to prophesy under the Old Testament law? Who served God? Who spoke for God? How did the outpouring of the Spirit change all of this?

2. What six different roles does God identify His people by in Acts chapter 2? Is there any contradiction between these

six different roles? Why or why not? What things does Acts 2 say believers shall do? Why do we need to see ourselves as servants?

3. What type of servants are spoken of in Acts 2? Why were these servants so-called? What did these types of servants do? When we take this in a spiritual context, who are handmaidens and menservants the servants of? What are we being prepared for?

4. What laws guided handmaidens and menservants? What happened if a servant desired to stay with their master for life? What did this make their service? How did life-long servants of God in the Bible acknowledge their mothers?

5. What were menservants and handmaidens willing to do? What quality did menservants and handmaidens have about them? What were they known for having?

6. What will a true handmaiden and menservant be ready for? Do they look for opportunities to serve? Why or why not? What do they do when their master is late in coming or is busy elsewhere? How does this attitude relate to the spiritual menservant or handmaiden? What do they do while awaiting new orders?

7. Who are two women who displayed the power of being a handmaiden? What did they do when faced with their impossible situations? What happens when we are God's handmaidens and menservants?

8. Who were two women who identified themselves as being "handmaidens of the Lord?" Why did they identify in this way? What do both show us about being servants?

9. What are some attitudes of menservants and handmaidens?

10. Who were some notable handmaidens and menservants in history?

11. Discuss and share some of the questions and answers found in the "Questions and Answers" section. What did you learn that you did not know about handmaidens and menservants? What did you learn that changed your mind about an opinion you might have had prior about handmaidens and menservants? How did learning about specific issues related to handmaidens and menservants help you to grow in your understanding of handmaiden and menservants? The church? Your own relationship with God?

12. Who is your favorite menservant or handmaiden? Why are they your favorite?

Nine ● SCRIBE

I write to mend
those places that got
snagged, ripped or frayed
while being human,
with other humans...
– Erika Harris, "Why I Write"[1]

N O one can question the history of writing and the power of the printed word. Writing was highly influential in the Protestant Reformation, in the press of the Pentecostal Movement, and yes, even in the letters of old, which were circulated among churches to become the New Testament epistles. Writing has been an important art form that has ensured the church's information be not only circulated in its immediate day, but last for subsequent generations down to the present day.

An important and often forgotten function is the work of the scribe, the writers who convey important revelation, facts, and information to people. It was done in the natural as a profession and in the spiritual by those who wrote for the Lord (and sometimes used professional scribes to take their dictation, as well). As a result, the scribes were the Biblical scholars of their time, highly knowledgeable of the words of Scripture and the ways the laws were interpreted (some even believe Jesus Himself was a scribe). Whether taking dictation or writing the revelation God gives to them Himself, the scribe conveys everything that needs saying in written form (either letters, books, or in ancient times, scrolls). In an age that is very visual and often foregoes written words for pictures, this chapter will reveal why the written word is so vital, and the function of the scribe so important, generation after generation (even in our own).

We should also take note that scribes were more than just writers. They were trusted individuals who not only took dictation, but had great understanding of the law and of the Scriptures. They knew how to do many things, do them well, and serve in their positions that often caused them great risk. As brave souls who show what a task writing is, the scribe introduces us to a powerful world of intellect, understanding, and shows that God loves the thinker and scholar as much as He loves everyone else.

TEXT STUDY

Jeremiah 36:1-32

POWER TEXTS

1 Chronicles 2:54-55, 1 Chronicles 24:6-19, 2 Chronicles 34:8-13, Nehemiah 13:10-14, Jeremiah 8:8-9, Matthew 23:27-36, Mark 3:14-30, Mark 12:28-34, John 3:1-21, Acts 5:33-42, Acts 22:1-5.

POWER VERSE

Jeremiah 36:32:

- *"Then took Jeremiah another roll, and gave it to Baruch the scribe, the son of Neriah; who wrote therein from the mouth of Jeremiah all the words of the book which Jehoiakim king of Judah had burned in the fire: and there were added besides unto them many like words."*

- *"So Jeremiah took another scroll and dictated again to his secretary, Baruch. He wrote everything that had been on the scroll King Jehoiakim had burned in the fire. Only this time he added much more!"* (NLT)

- *"Then Jeremiah took another scroll and dictated again to Baruch all he had written before, only this time the Lord added a lot more!"* (TLB)

- *"Then Jeremiah took another scroll and gave it to Baruch the scribe, the son of Neri'ah, who wrote on it at the dictation of Jeremiah all the words of the scroll which Jehoi'akim king of Judah had burned in the fire; and many similar words were added to them."* (RSV)

- *"Then Jeremiah took another scroll and gave it to Baruch the scribe, the son of Neriah, who wrote on it at the dictation of Jeremiah all the words of the book which Jehoiakim king of Judah had burned in the fire; and besides them many similar words were added."* (AMP)

- *"And Jeremiah hath taken another roll, and giveth it unto Baruch son of Neriah the scribe, and he writeth on it from the mouth of Jeremiah all the words of the book that Jehoiakim king of Judah hath burnt in the fire; and again there were added unto them many words like these."* (YLT)

POWER WORDS

- **Jeremiah** – From the Hebrew word *Yirmeyah* which means, "Jeremiah = whom Jehovah has appointed; the major prophet, son of Hilkiah of the priestly family in Anathoth; author of the prophetic book bearing his name; a man of Libnah and father of Hamutal the wife of king Josiah; a Gadite who joined David at Ziklag; a Manassehite, one of the mighty men of valour of the Transjordanic half tribe of Manasseh; a Gadite and warrior of David; a warrior of David; a priest who joined Nehemiah in the covenant ceremony; a priest also in the time of Nehemiah; maybe same as 7; father of Jaazaniah the Rechabites."[2]

- **Roll** – From the Hebrew word *megillah* which means "roll, book, writing."[3]

- **Baruch** – From the Hebrew word *Baruwk* which means, "blessed; friend, amanuensis, and faithful attendant of Jeremiah; a priest, the son of Zabbai who assisted Nehemiah in rebuilding the walls of Jerusalem 3) a priest, or family of priests, who signed the covenant with Nehemiah 4) son of Col-hozeh, a descendant of Perez or Pharez, the son of Judah."[4]

- **Scribe** – From the Hebrew word *caphar,* which means, "to count, recount, relate, to count (things), to number, take account of, reckon, to be counted, be numbered, to recount, rehearse, declare, to recount (something), rehearse, to talk, to count exactly or accurately, to be recounted, be rehearsed, be related; enumerator, muster-officer, secretary, scribe, enumerator, muster-officer, secretary, learned man, scribe."[5]

- **Neriah** – From the Hebrew word *Neriyah* which means, "Neriah = lamp of Jehovah; son of Maaseiah and father of Baruch and Seraiah."[6]

- **Wrote** – From the Hebrew word *kathab* which means "to write, record, enroll."[7]

- **Mouth** – From the Hebrew word *peh* which means "mouth."[8]

- **Book** – From the Hebrew word *cepher* which means "book; missive, document, writing, book."[9]

- **Jehoiakim** – From the Hebrew word *Yehowyaqiym* which means "Jehovah raises up; son of Josiah and the third from the last king of Judah; subject vassel of Nebuchadnezzar who reigned for 11 years before he died a violent death either in combat or by the hands of his own subjects."[10]

- **Burned** – From the Hebrew word *saraph* which means "to burn."[11]

- **Added** – From the Hebrew word *yacaph* which means "to add, increase, do again."[12]

- **Words** – From the Hebrew word *dabar* which means "speech, word, speaking, thing."[13]

HISTORICAL CONTEXT

The scribes of old were multi-faceted people who had access to every important secular, governmental, and spiritual event in existence. Without tape recorders, digital software, and computers, dictations were done by hand. When something needed to be remembered, recorded, remunerated, or memorized, it was the scribe who was called in. They had so much experience with reading and re-reading documents, they became scholars and teachers of the law and of governmental and educational practices, proving the connection between visually seeing, hearing, and writing down information. The scribe was forever where it was at, as the official jack-of-all professional trades as related to law, Scripture, writing, understanding, and revelation.

NOTES ON TEXT

When it was time to write the words of the revelation to the people, the first person the Prophet Jeremiah called was Baruch, a scribe. Baruch didn't just write the words; he read them and preserved them, as well. Walking in obedience, Baruch did everything Jeremiah commanded of him to the point of being at risk along with the prophet when the king burned the scroll. When the king was out of the way for rejecting the scroll, the Prophet Jeremiah called once again on Baruch to be there, as a faithful worker, and write the words again, with new ones added.

POWER POINTS

- Scribes were the writers of their day. More than just writers, scribes were positioned both in sacred posts and in secular or governmental ones, as well. They were the individuals who calculated, who counted, who called to attention, who kept records, who took dictation, who edited, who read what was written, who wrote their own words, and who kept the sacred records of Scripture and prophetic review. From their experience with writing and re-writing the Words of God, scribes were serious scholars of the Scriptures and the law, extremely well-versed in its literal context and in its interpretation, as well (Nehemiah 13:10-14). The Scriptures indicate there were many scribes in the Old Testament who were also Levites, thus showing the important emphasis of education in priestly and ministry work (1 Chronicles 2:54-55, 1 Chronicles 24:6-19, 2 Chronicles 34:8-13).

- Scribes were trustworthy people, individuals who could be trusted with the important, the confidential, the governmental, and the sacred. If something happened legally or politically as pertains to the document, the scribe would have the same weight of responsibility as the person who gave the dictation, if that was a different individual. Scribes were as responsible for carrying and relaying messages they wrote as the individuals who wrote them (given it may have been a different person) (Jeremiah 36:1-32).

- In the New Testament, "scribes" were also called "teachers of the law." This means the view given to scribes in the New Testament was mixed, especially in relationship to Jesus. It was not so much the work of the scribe that Jesus condemned, but those scribes who had gained such a narrow perspective of the law and their understanding that they had lost sight of the One Whom they served (Mark 3:14-30). Through the arguments of eroded scribes, Jesus proved that their understandings of the Scriptures were incomplete. We are warned of such people in the Old Testament as well (Jeremiah 8:8-9): we should never trust false interpretations of things or false copies of spiritual matters, no matter how wise they may sound or how much they may sound like a law of God, because there will always be people who will reject the word of the Lord.

- Jesus' perspectives on the scribes was not entirely negative (and we must avoid the temptation to generalize the role of the scribe as bad or inherently evil, because we can see the scribe performs many important functions). It was a scribe who He told was not far from the Kingdom of God because he recognized the greatest of all the commandments (Mark 12:28-34). Nicodemus was a scribe, and Nicodemus was one that Jesus spoke to at length about essential aspects to salvation, because He knew Nicodemus could understand them (John 3:1-21).

- Jesus also states that He would send to the evil scribes and Pharisees true prophets, scribes, and teachers (Matthew 23:27-36). This shows us the true and important nature of education in ministry, in church, in teaching, in the study of the Word, and also opens the door for every scribal work that can exist in the church, including theologians, apologetics, professors, and academic schools for seminary and higher theological learning. It is not in competition with faith to be knowledgeable; rather, Jesus said He was sending out the scholars in the form of the scribes!

- Many today ignore the work of the scribe in the early church and especially in the life of the Apostle Paul. We learn that his education in the law was under the work of Gamaliel, a scribe (Acts 22:1-5). Gamaliel also addressed the Sanhedrin council on behalf of the apostles, and persuaded the rulers to set the apostles free after flogging rather than killing them. It was his careful knowledge of the law that helped the early church to spread, and preserved God's workers through another siege with the law (Acts 5:33-42).

WAYS WE CAN UTILIZE THE SCRIBE FUNCTION

Scribes are vital to the function of the church. Without them, true knowledge of the Bible and Biblical understanding do not exist and we would not have the ability to train and teach within the church. Unfortunately, however, the work of the scribes is often minimized in the face of more entertaining work, such as preaching. Here are some ways we can better utilize the scribal function and how it can better our lives of faith.

- **Purchase their books and materials** – Scribes are often, first and foremost, known for their ability to write and convey important ideas. If a scribe has a book available, get a copy of that book. Don't ask for it for free or that you are given a copy, because that doesn't show support for their work. If a scribe has another work they are doing in addition, whether it is professionally or spiritually, support that. Appreciate the knowledge base the scribe has.

- **Enroll in a class or in an educational endeavor** – It's hard for those with scribes' abilities today because people don't want to learn. Believing that gifts compensate where abilities lack, people reject the idea of being educated and learning. This is not God's way! The reason we have people who are so knowledgeable in things is so they can educate others so we can all be educated. Embrace the abilities of the scribe in seminary, writing, classes, and study Bibles.

- **Embrace different abilities** – I have said for years that not everyone who is in ministry is a preacher. Preaching is a great ability and a powerful work, but not everyone is supposed to do that. There are lots of different gifts, works, and abilities within the church that we need to embrace and accept. We need to stop thinking in a box and start opening up our minds to learn of the wondrous things that God wants us to study and explore if we will only allow ourselves to be taught.

SCRIBES IN HISTORY

The work of the scribes throughout history speaks for itself as they have written and taught through the ages. Here are some scribes who have made a Kingdom impact right down to the present day.

- **William Tyndale (1494-1536)** – Did you know that the majority of the King James Bible translation was actually William Tyndale's? William Tyndale was an English scholar. We know little about his early life, but we do know that he graduated from Oxford and worked intensely to study Biblical languages and study theology and Scripture. He found himself frequently at odds with the rest of clergy due to his views, which were considered radical at the time. As a dissenter from Catholic ideals, he believed it was important to make the Bible available in the language of the people. William Tyndale's work was the first English Bible to draw directly from the Hebrew and Greek, the first to utilize the printing press on a large scale, and one of the first Bible translations of the Reformation. His work on Biblical translation not only significantly impacted Christianity, it also impacted the English language. He was later betrayed and beheaded for heresy…but his impact clearly lives on.[14]

- **John Foxe (1516/17-1587)** – Most of us have heard of *Foxe's Book of Martyrs*, but we don't know much of the man behind the book. John Foxe was a historian and martyrologist whose book on martyrology shaped the way Protestants viewed faith for centuries. He was born in England and was a very devout and scholarly child from a very young age. After becoming a Protestant in 1545, John Foxe resigned his college position and went on to experience life as a dissenter from popular views, unto having and experiencing severe financial hardship. Even though many of his views would be archaic today, none of us can question the vital work we have through *Foxe's Book of Martyrs*, which he started in 1552 and gave a startling view of the experiences of Christian martyrs throughout the centuries.[15]

- **Anne Dutton (1692-1765)** – Anne Dutton survived a severe childhood illness and went on to receive a strong religious education. After being widowed after five years of marriage and then her second husband's return ship was lost at sea, she still worked and persevered to write theological inspirations in her time. A powerful poet and writer on religion, Anne Dutton released fifty books in her lifetime. She also corresponded with George Whitefield and John Wesley.[16]

- **Sarah Osborn (1714-1796)** – We know from Sarah Osborn's history that she kept journals throughout her life, and we are able to see that her great spiritual inspiration came from living through the Great Awakening. Even though she struggled before this point, she used her faith to persevere and eventually write *Familiar Letters*, which details her great faith and inspiration for faith.[17]

QUESTIONS AND ANSWERS

- **How can we relate the scribal work in our modern times?**

  The work of scribes is multi-faceted and that means it is always and forever relevant. The work of scribes is an intellectual one, something that crosses from written arts to theology to practical instruction and other forms of academics. This means that the work of the scribe is an educational one, as it seeks to draw out and reach out to people through information. Scribes are our apologists, our theologians, our seminarians, and our educators. They are people who take written words about faith and research about spiritual things and turn them into books, courses, research materials, and yes, even sermons or speeches. This essential work is the foundation to Christian academics and education, and that is true, even in our modern day and age.

- **Why the emphasis on education? Shouldn't we be more interested in the Spirit?**

  The competition between education and the Spirit does not exist in the Bible. It is a more recent attack that has developed in modern times to create additional conflict between the world (which education is seen as being) and the church. For centuries, the church has recognized the importance of having educated clergy and educated members. Yes, there are people who believe that education alone equips a leader for ministry and for church service, but I am not advocating that. I know that if a minister does not have the Spirit, they will not be effective in ministry. But I also think we need to acknowledge that not being properly educated is also hurting ministers just as much as not having the Spirit. There are many leaders who might be energetic, interested, enthusiastic, even very

Spirit-filled, but who go nowhere in ministry because they do not have the education to present the Gospel and present their ministries in the way they need to in order for their ministries to take off. Ministers need both education and the Spirit, which is why we need scribes to help educate the church where needed and inspire truth and promise to the general body of believers.

- **What is the difference between a scribe and a teacher?**

The New Testament indicates that teachers are a part of the five-fold ministry. How a teacher may teach varies greatly. They may or may not teach a class, they may teach in a church setting or in a Christian school, or in other forums such as working to build textbooks or curriculum. On the surface, the work of the scribe sounds similar, but there are differences. The first difference is that a scribe is a function, rather than an office. The second difference is that teaching is more interactive with people as a rule than the work of the scribe. While a teacher might publically teach a class, a scribe might have written the book they use in that class. A teacher might teach a congregation, while a scribe might teach in a seminary, working more with future ministers or leaders than a teacher does. It is completely possible for a teacher to function as a scribe, while a scribe may not always function as a teacher. It may also be something done for a period of time by someone and then never done again. When one is a teacher, it is something that person does, consistently, throughout their lives.

- **Can women be scribes?**

Yes, there is nothing to suggest that they can't, and history proves women have functioned in this along with men.

- **What is the difference between a scribe and a Pharisee, since the two were often mentioned together in the New Testament?**

The position or office of a Pharisee was something man-made that emerged in Jesus' time because they believed the exile leading up to Jesus' time was caused by Israel's disobedience to the law. They were considered guardians of the Law, put into place to make sure that the Israelites didn't fall or fail again. The problem with this, as we can see in Jesus' dialogues with them, is that they did cause people to fall. It became an issue of power and control rather than true understanding of the Law and moral guidance.

The work of the scribes was Biblical, as we can see throughout the Old Testament. Rather than being there to keep people from error, the scribes were scholars who understood how to interpret the law. They often served as advocates to interpretation, they helped judge the law, and they helped in the interpretation of it. While it is obvious that the Pharisees and scribes did work together, they did have two separate works and two different purposes.

- **What makes a scribe different from a secretary?**

In a certain sense, a scribe does do some things that are similar to the work of a secretary, but a scribe is much more than just a secretary. They do all of the things we have spoken of throughout this chapter, including study, interpretation, scholarship, instruction, research, writing, public reading, calculating, assessing, numbering, and educating. They are not just assistants to someone else or to someone else on earth, but are professionals in the work of God.

DISCUSSION, STUDY AND REVIEW QUESTIONS

1. What things did the scribes of old have access to? When was a scribe called in to a situation? How did they become the teachers and scholars of the Old Testament Law? What professional areas belonged to the scribes?

2. When it was time to write down the words of revelation, who was the first person Jeremiah called on? What did Baruch do besides writing down the words? What happened to Baruch as a result of being involved in this project? What happened after the situation resolved itself?

3. In their day, what did scribes do? Is this all they did? What else did they do? Why were they serious scholars of the Old Testament? Were there Levites who were also scribes? Why is this relevant?

4. What kind of people were scribes? What were some of their responsibilities?

5. What other term refers to scribes that is found in the New Testament? Why was the view of scribes mixed in the New Testament? What did Jesus condemn about many of the scribes of His day? What did Jesus prove among the scribes who were in error? Should we be wary of false scribes? Why or why not?

6. Was Jesus' view on the scribes entirely negative? Why or why not? Who was a notable scribe who was important in the ministry of Jesus? Why was he important?

7. What did Jesus say He would send to evil scribes and Pharisees? What does this say to us? What does it open the door to for all of us? What does it tell us about the church and education?

8. Who did the Apostle Paul study under before he became an apostle? What did this individual do for the early apostles of the church? Why was he qualified to help in this situation?

9. What are some ways we can utilize the scribe's function?

10. Who were some notable scribes in history?

11. Discuss and share some of the questions and answers found in the "Questions and Answers" section. What did you learn that you did not know about scribes? What did you learn that changed your mind about an opinion you might have had prior about scribes? How did learning about specific issues related to scribes help you to grow in your understanding of scribes? The church? Your own relationship with God?

12. Who is your favorite scribe? Why are they your favorite?

Ten ● Spiritual Father and Mother

Tell me and I'll forget.
Show me and I'll remember.
Involve me and I'll understand.
– Confucius[1]

WHEN I was growing up, I never heard the term "spiritual mother" or "spiritual father." It was something I started to hear about as an adult, in church, long after I was an ordained minister. I came up in my adult faith life hearing about pastors, about covering, every now and then we might have heard about evangelists or prophets, but nobody ever used the term. Fast-forward twenty years, now everyone seems to be talking about their "spiritual parents." Whether it is a man, a woman, or a man and a woman both, having spiritual parentage is the new "it" thing that seems to be very important to many people.

The truth is that the role of a spiritual father or mother is often an important one, because it is foundational. Because it is so foundational, that also makes it rare and something that we only experience a few times in our lives. Since it is not uncommon for people to list that they have several dozen sets of spiritual parents (which is not reasonable), it's important that we understand what it means to be a spiritual parent, and what exactly spiritual fathers and mothers do within our spiritual lives.

TEXT STUDY

1 Corinthians 4:14-21

POWER TEXTS

Genesis 45:4-11, Judges 4:1-5:9, Judges 17:1-13, 2 Samuel 20:14-22, 2 Kings 2:1-12, Ezekiel 16:44-48, John 19:25-27, Galatians 4:17-31, 1 Thessalonians 2:7-12, 1 Peter 3:1-7, 1 John 2:12-14.

POWER VERSE

1 Corinthians 4:15:

- *"For though ye have ten thousand instructors in Christ, yet have ye not many fathers: for in Christ Jesus I have begotten you through the gospel."*

- *"For if ye should have ten thousand instructors in Christ, yet not many fathers; for in Christ Jesus I have begotten you through the glad tidings."* (DARBY)

- *"For though you may have ten thousand teachers [guardians; tutors] in Christ, you do not have many father. [For; Because] Through the Good News [Gospel] I became your father in Christ Jesus."* (EXB)

- *"For even if you had ten thousand others to teach you about Christ, you have only one spiritual father. For I became your father in Christ Jesus when I preached the Good News to you."* (NLT)

- *"For though you may have ten thousand guardians in Christ, you do not have many fathers, because I became your father in Christ Jesus through the Gospel."* (NET)

- *"For though you may have ten thousand mentors in Christ, but you don't have many fathers. I gave birth to you in Christ Jesus through the Gospel."* (CEB)

POWER WORDS

- **Ten thousand** – From the Greek word *murioi* which means, "innumerable, countless; ten thousand."[2]

- **Instructors** – From the Greek word *paidagogos* which means "a tutor i.e. a guardian and guide of boys. Among the Greeks and the Romans the name was applied to trustworthy slaves who were charged with the duty of supervising the life and morals of boys belonging to the better class. The boys were not allowed so much as to step out of the house without them before arriving at the age of manhood."[3]

- **Fathers** – From the Greek word *pater* which means, "generator or male ancestor; metaph. the originator and transmitter of anything, the authors of a family or society of persons animated by the same spirit as himself, one who has infused his own spirit into others, who actuates and governs their minds, one who stands in a father's place and looks after another in a paternal way, a title of honour, teachers, as those to whom pupils trace back the knowledge and training they have received, the members of the Sanhedrin, whose prerogative it was by virtue of the wisdom and experience in which they excelled, to take charge of the interests of others; God is called the Father."[4]

- **Begotten** – From the Greek word *gennao*, which means, "of men who fathered children, to be born, to be begotten, of women giving birth to children; metaph. to engender, cause to arise, excite, in a Jewish sense, of one who brings others over to his way of life, to convert someone, of God making Christ His son, of God making men his sons through faith in Christ's work."[5]

- **Gospel** – From the Greek word *euaggelion* which means, "a reward for good tidings; good tidings, the glad tidings of the kingdom of God soon to be set up, and subsequently also of Jesus the Messiah, the founder of this kingdom. After the death of Christ, the term comprises also the preaching of (concerning) Jesus Christ as having suffered death on the cross to procure eternal salvation for the men in the kingdom of God, but as restored to life and exalted to the right hand of God in heaven, thence to return in majesty to consummate the kingdom of God, the glad tidings of salvation through Christ, the proclamation of the grace of God manifest and pledged in Christ, the gospel, as the messianic rank of Jesus was proved by his words, his deeds, and his death, the narrative of the sayings, deeds, and death of Jesus Christ came to be called the gospel or glad tidings."[6]

HISTORICAL CONTEXT

In Biblical times, one's line of teaching and school of thought was intimately related to who the leader or individual was that taught them in that school of thought. It was believed that a teacher was an originating point in their life, of a new start and of birthing something forth in that individual within their minds and life growth and development. Because the way a person thought and believed represented the way one lived, it was almost as if someone was renewed, or had a new parentage, in their lives.

NOTES ON TEXT

It is obvious that in New Testament times, the church faced many of the same problems that relate to authority that we do in modern times. Even though there might have been thousands of people who claimed to be teachers and tried to take credit for where someone was in the faith, the Apostle Paul was quick to clarify that no matter how many people might teach, he was the originator of their faith, their father in the Gospel, because they were birthed forth from his instruction.

POWER POINTS

- Spiritual mothers and fathers (collectively called spiritual parenting) is the process by which a man or a woman in the faith is in some way an originator or foundational teacher in your life by which your faith is built. This is distinguished from a general teacher or leader in your life who you may care about and who may bless you, but is not foundational. They may be foundational in the sense of your initial Christian faith or foundational in the sense of a ministry, a calling, or another spiritual purpose. However they come into your life, they present something that originates from their teaching and guides you through the remainder of your Christian walk (1 Corinthians 4:14-21). They are people who are important to us, forever remembered, and forever essential as we walk forward and take what they taught us with them (2 Kings 2:1-12).

- Spiritual parentage calls upon our lineage of faith (Galatians 4:17-31, 1 Peter 3:1-7). If we imitate the way of faith that our ancestors had, then we are a part of their spiritual heritage, and they are our progenitors of faith. They have laid an essential foundation so we are able to believe, even today.

- Spiritual mothers and fathers show God's love to us and also show us how important connections are in the Kingdom. Anyone can teach us things, but not everyone has the ability to form essential relationship and train us in a foundational sense. Spiritual parents help us develop both faith and character, disciplining us when necessary (1 Corinthians 4:14-21). They care for us, about us, and take interest in us as people. They know the impact of the Gospel, and live it for us in our lives, working to make sure it is real to us (1 John 2:12-14). As a result, they see us grow in the faith and are able to encourage, comfort, and urge us to live holy and worthy for God (1 Thessalonians 2:7-12). In turn, we too make the commitment to our spiritual parents, treating them as we even would our natural parents (John 19:25-27). We should make the commitment to see to it that they too have what they need and to love them as our own family.

- Spiritual parentage always has a purpose. Through strong guidance and leadership, spiritual parentage has changed the state of nations and the state of spiritual lives alike. As a result of spiritual parentage, battles are won (Judges 4:1-5:9). Even though it might seem strange or not make sense to people, there is always a purpose that God has in connecting people with their spiritual parents (Genesis 45:4-11). That connection is long-term, not short and sweet. The season of spiritual parentage lasts a long time.

- We are commanded to be careful who we take on as our spiritual parents in our lives, because as our spiritual parents are known, so too we become known. We should never seek out those who mislead spiritually or who mislead on things as pertain to the natural realm, either (Judges 17:1-13, Ezekiel 16:44-48).

- As spiritual seats of influence, cities in Israel were sometimes called "mother cities." This indicated not only their importance in a national sense, but also in a spiritual one. Things that were spiritual happened and came down in a spiritually legal sense from these locations (2 Samuel 20:14-22). In the same sense, the Bible speaks of the New Jerusalem in heaven as being our mother, because it is a source from which God's truth and worship shall come (Galatians 4:26-27).

WAYS WE CAN HONOR SPIRITUAL MOTHERS AND FATHERS

Spiritual mothers and fathers sow much into our lives in many different ways, and we are truly indebted to them as their spiritual children. Since we have so few of them in our lives, we should pay tribute to them. Here are some ways we can do just that, and acknowledge their impact.

- **Recognize appreciation ceremonies** – There is debate about appreciation, pastoral and ministerial anniversary, and church anniversary celebrations. Some people argue it's idol worship or leader worship, and other people feel it is absolutely necessary. I think the Bible teaches us that our leaders are worthy of double honor, and if we consider the sacrifices that people in ministry make for their ministries, it is absolutely imperative that those who benefit from their ministries show appreciation to them and give the opportunity to celebrate their appreciation in some form. If your spiritual parents are in ministry, acknowledge and participate in their appreciation services.

- **Say "thank you" and communicate your appreciation to them** – As one who has been a spiritual parent to many, the few that come back and tell us how grateful they are for what we have done for them are a limited number. Let your spiritual parents know they are important to you. Don't forget about them in acknowledgements and memories.

- **Live what they have taught you** – The best thanks a spiritual parent can get is to see the individual they have invested time and education in walk in the faith as God has called and blessed them. There is no greater joy than seeing a spiritual child serve God.

SPIRITUAL MOTHERS AND FATHERS IN HISTORY

Spiritual mothers and fathers have manifested in different ways throughout history. Here is our tribute to but a handful of them, and the lasting difference they made for the Kingdom.

- **Desert Fathers (3rd to 5th centuries)** – The Desert Fathers were individuals who led early monastic communities that were weary of worldly life and sought to establish communities of spirituality and spiritual disciplines in the deserts of Egypt. The spiritual mysticism, emphasis on charity, forgiveness, reciting scripture, meditation, and rejecting society became major themes for Christians for centuries; if not in whole, in part. They also had many spiritual children, both sons and daughters, who sought their advice and who they trained and reared up in essential spiritual ways.[7]

- **Desert mothers (4th and 5th centuries)** – Among the works of the Desert Fathers, there are only a handful of women who are mentioned: Amma Syncletica of Alexandria, Theodoria of Alexandria, Amma Sarah of the Desert, Melania the Elder, Melania the Younger, Olympias, Saint Paula, her daughter Eustochium, and several other women who are not named. I am including them here as a group because they are so deeply important to the history of Christian tradition, justice does not serve if we ignore the Desert Mothers. They led groups of men and women, taught, and provided true spiritual parentage to many who were weary of worldly life and sought refuge and depth in desert places.[8]

- **Savvas the Spiritual Father of Ioannina (d. 1505)** – Savvas was born of noble birth, although we are not sure where he was from or where he lived. We do know that he desired to imitate Christ in every way possible, and spent most of his life as a hermit. He dealt constantly with spiritual warfare, and sought more sincerely to discipline himself spiritually. He was so well-known for his life and for his spiritual disciplines that crowds sought him out to teach from him and receive his spiritual parentage. His famous statement was "The foundation stone of the spiritual life is humility." For the many years that he worked and taught with them, he was reported to never lose his temper or judge another, as he kept himself so well grounded in humility.[9]

- **Susanna Wesley (1669-1742)** – Susanna Wesley, known as the "Mother of Methodism," was the mother of John and Charles Wesley, both of whom were heavily involved in the founding of the Methodist Church. Despite many hardships throughout her life (including an abusive and abandoning husband and a house fire), Susanna Wesley sought to educate all of her children herself, and also started her own home church. At one point in time, over two hundred people attended her Sunday afternoon service while service at conventional churches slowly shrunk. She practiced devotion, believed fervently for the devotion and sanctity of her children, and never gave up on the promise of the grace of God.[10]

QUESTIONS AND ANSWERS

- **Can godparents be considered spiritual parents?**

Since godparents are traditionally assigned to a child to assist in bringing that child up and especially assisting and directing their faith formation, godparents who fill this role (who are more than just ceremonially selected and are genuinely involved) can definitely fill the role of being spiritual parents in one's life.

- **Does every spiritual leader we have qualify as a spiritual mother or father?**

  No. While some spiritual leaders we have might be great people and might help us to develop spiritually in some way, spiritual parentage is limited to those who have made a foundational or progenitor-like influence in our lives. While every leader might teach us something new or help us learn things, that does not make every leader we have a spiritual parent.

- **How many spiritual parents can we have?**

  I have seen people pay tribute to important women in their lives and thank God for their seven or eight or ten spiritual mothers. This is a bit much, and a real misappropriation of what a spiritual mother or father is. In our lives, we are lucky if we have a handful of spiritual parents (maybe two or three). We don't get dozens of spiritual parents, especially at the same time. The short answer is that we get as many spiritual parents as we need. The more involved answer is that in our lives, we don't get that many.

- **Can we have a single spiritual parent?**

  Yes. Spiritual parents don't always follow earthly patterns, and it is possible to have a man or a woman be a spiritual parent to you by themselves. We use the term "spiritual parents" not to indicate that every spiritual parent you have is married to one another, but to designate that a spiritual parent can be either a woman or a man, and also because most of us will have at least one male and one female spiritual parent in our lifetimes.

- **Are spiritual parents always ministers?**

  I think that while many spiritual parents are in ministry (and they may be our first pastors, our first ministry coverings, or a special ministry covering to us), not all spiritual parents are ministers. Sometimes they are just faithful people (like the example of godparents earlier) who cared enough about us to make sure we were in faith and were properly given the foundation we need in our faith.

- **Do we ever outgrow spiritual parents?**

  If we are progressing in our faith like we are supposed to be, it is likely that, with all things that relate to spirituality, there will probably come a time when our relationship with our spiritual parents will change. Even though they may still be in our lives, we will move to a new area or to different spiritual places where someone else will be more qualified to take over in our development. There is also the possibility that spiritual parents may die or transition in our lives in another way. Just like natural parents, however, that doesn't mean we need to ignore them or pretend they don't exist. We can always appreciate what they have done for us, even if new leadership takes a place in our lives.

DISCUSSION, STUDY AND REVIEW QUESTIONS

1. In Biblical times, how did different schools of thought relate to their instructors or founders? What did people believe about their instructors? How did this relate to spiritual parentage?

2. Did the church of the New Testament have some of the same problems that we have today? How can we see this? Even though there might have been many teachers, what did the Apostle Paul clarify for us? Why was the Apostle Paul the only one out of all those teachers who was qualified to be their spiritual father?

3. What are spiritual mothers and fathers? How is this distinguished from a teacher or other person who might be an important leader in your life? How might a spiritual mother or father be foundational in your life? What do they represent in your life? How are they important to us?

4. How does spiritual parentage call on our ancestors in the faith? Why is this important?

5. How do spiritual mothers and fathers reflect God's love and show us important Kingdom connections? How do spiritual parents help us develop faith and character? What commitment do we make to our spiritual parents?

6. Does spiritual parentage always have a purpose? Why or why not? How does spiritual parentage change events outside of us? How long is the connection to a spiritual parent?

7. Why should we be careful about who are spiritual parents are? Should we ever seek out those who mislead about spiritual or life matters? Why or why not?

8. Why were cities sometimes known as "mother cities?" What does this term tell us about them? Why is the New Jerusalem spoken of as our "mother?"

9. What are some ways we can honor our spiritual mothers and fathers?

10. Who were some notable spiritual mothers and fathers in history?

11. Discuss and share some of the questions and answers found in the "Questions and Answers" section. What did you learn that you did not know about spiritual mothers

and fathers? What did you learn that changed your mind about an opinion you might have had prior about spiritual mothers and fathers? How did learning about specific issues related to spiritual mothers and fathers help you to grow in your understanding of spiritual mothers and fathers? The church? Your own relationship with God?

12. Who is your favorite spiritual mother or father? Why are they your favorite?

Eleven ● CHURCH MOTHER

A mother's love is the fuel that enables a normal human being to do the impossible.
– Sayings for Church Signs[1]

THE role of the church mother is one that people recall with mixed feelings and mixed memories. Some people loved church mothers and feel that we need to bring church mothers back with a vengeance in our modern times. They believe that church mothers helped train up young women, helped keep modesty in the church, helped keep women active and involved in church ministries, and attended to the helps and needs of a ministry. Others see the role of church mothers in a radically different light. There are many who viewed the more traditional concepts of church mothers as being mean, nasty, controlling, fowl-mouthed, judgmental, and arrogant. In the experiences of many people, church mothers were trying to enforce traditional values, but did so with a bad attitude and took liberties in the process with their words and behavior because they felt they were of a certain age and knew they could get away with it. The result of such staunch and unrelenting unkindness was seen in young women who tended to run away from church and gravitate toward all sorts of worldly things and desires.

The truth about church mothers is that they evolved as sort of a ministry compensation for refusing to ordain women or allow them to participate as equals in the work of the church. When a woman was of a certain age, she was considered a "church mother" and fulfilled certain roles without credentials and without the rite of ordination. The work of the "First Lady" (pastor's wife) was also out of this same tradition, where the pastor's wife of a church often fulfilled the duties of a female leader, without the formal pastoral acknowledgements.

Church mothers are worth a look, no matter how or why they started. First Ladies are also worth a look, especially in the tradition of the church mother. Here we are going to see how this function of the church can expand and improve, especially for our modern times.

TEXT STUDY

Titus 2:3-8

POWER TEXTS

Genesis 3:20, Proverbs 6:20-22, Proverbs 11:15-18, Proverbs 14:1-5, Proverbs 31:1-31, Isaiah 66:10-13, Matthew 12:46-50, Matthew 27:55-61, 2 Timothy 1:3-7, 1 Timothy 5:1-8, 2 John 1:1-6.

POWER VERSE

Titus 2:3:

- *"The aged women likewise, that they be in behavior as becometh holiness, not false accusers, not given to much wine, teachers of good things..."*

- *"Older women likewise are to be reverent in behavior, not slanderers or slaves to much wine. They are to teach what is good..."* (ESV)

- *"In the same way, teach older women to be holy [reverent] in their behavior, not speaking against [slandering; gossiping about] others or enslaved to too much wine [excessive drinking], but teaching what is good..."* (EXB)

- *"Teach the older women to be quiet and respectful in everything they do. They must not go around speaking evil of others and must not be heavy drinkers, but they should be teachers of goodness."* (TLB)

- *"Older women likewise are to exhibit behavior fitting for those who are holy, not slandering, not slaves to excessive drinking, but teaching what is good."* (NET)

- *"Bid the older women likewise to be reverent in behavior, not to be slanderers or slaves to drink; they are to teach what is good..."* (RSV)

POWER WORDS

- **Aged women** – From the Greek word *presbutis* which means, "an aged woman."[2]

- **Behavior** – From the Greek word *katastema* which means "demeanour, deportment, bearing."[3]

- **Becometh holiness** – From the Greek word *hieroprepes* which means, "befitting men, places, actions or sacred things to God; reverent."[4]

- **False accusers** – From the Greek word *diabolos* which means, "prone to slander, slanderous, accusing falsely; metaph. applied to a man who, by opposing the cause of God, may be said to act the part of the devil or to side with him."[5]

- **Given to much wine** – From three Greek words: *douloo* which means "to make a slave of, reduce to bondage; metaph. give myself wholly to one's needs and service, make myself a bondman to him"[6] *polus* which means " many, much, large"[7] and *oinos* which means "wine; metaph. fiery wine of God's wrath."[8]

- **Teachers of good things** – From the Greek word *kalodidaskalos* which means "teaching that which is good, a teacher of goodness."[9]

HISTORICAL CONTEXT

The world of the New Testament was, not unlike our world today, afloat with many different ways to do things, many different ways to live, and many different ideas about how to get things done. Radical for the time frame was the Apostle Paul's injunction for older women to take a leadership position in the church and teach about essential things that affected the lives and women and young men of their era. In cultures that abandoned older women as having no purpose because they could no longer have children, the Apostle Paul gave these women a purpose and a duty.

NOTES ON TEXT

The terminology "aged women" or "older women" is actually a term in the Greek to indicate "female elders." If we are to understand the work of the church mothers, they are often, in essence, councils of older women who are serving an eldership position to their churches and ministries. The Bible emphasizes the relevance of good character, behavior, and conduct among such women, because they are in a perfect situation to mentor and train younger members of a congregation.

POWER POINTS

- The term "church mother" is not found in the Bible. What we do find as we examine church mothers, however, are patterns of female eldership as is found in the New Testament (Titus 2:3-8). They are commanded to conduct themselves accordingly, representing the work of the elder as being reverent, not gossips or slandering other people, not given to drinking too much, and able to teach what is good. The female elders are encouraged to mentor the younger women, as good role models, and as women who can give advice and assistance in many different situations. Not just being subject to annoy or discipline others, they are encouraged to be teachers – to teach them about home life and family life, to encourage them to attend to the work that is at hand and not neglect their families, to help them adapt to the changes that come with having families, and to have good marriages. They are also called to encourage young men and encourage them to be self-controlled, showing them integrity, seriousness, good use of words and appropriate language, and making it so that there is nothing bad that can be said about any members of the church who are younger and coming into themselves. They stand as people, ready to pass on the faith as in the tradition of Eunice and Lois (2 Timothy 1:3-7).

- Church mothers follow in the tradition of Eve, who was proclaimed "Mother of all living" (Genesis 3:20). As a church mother, a woman has an opportunity to be a mother to the living, to those who are alive and redeemed in Christ. They also follow the tradition of recognizing that those who are in Christ are His family (Matthew 12:46-50). When we are in Him, we have many family members, and that includes church mothers. The church mother has the opportunity to nurture and comfort, support younger members of the church in their life changes, celebrate with their advances, and extend peace to all who cross her path (Isaiah 66:10-13).

- Church mothers should always remember that kindheartedness gains honor (Proverbs 11:15-18). Being overly harsh or critical with people will bring about undesirable results, because being cruel brings on ruin. By conveying the essential teachings of God with love and kindness, the church mother has the opportunity to make a lasting impact on the lives of others (Proverbs 6:20-22). Not every person in church has a good relationship with their own biological parents, thus church mothers have a great opportunity to offer spiritual support as is needed and show people they are loved, despite what they might have done or experienced in their lives.

- The work of a church mother centers around wisdom. When a woman is wise, she builds her own house. In the case of a church mother, she is building the house of the church to be strong and steady, and ensuring that future generations will also be present as they walk uprightly and honestly with the Lord and each other (Proverbs 14:1-5). They are there for the Lord, willing to be of service in any way that is needed within the community (Matthew 27:55-61). As a result, they too are able to receive and accept the honor they are due among the community (1 Timothy 5:1-8).

- Church mothers remind us all to be women who pursue excellence and virtue in our own lives, and they are women who have the opportunity to help us excel and become people in touch with our destinies. Many forget that the words of Proverbs 31 were given to King Lemuel by his mother, which means that she stood in a spiritual role and proclaimed words of righteousness and justice that affected both men and women (Proverbs 31:1-31). May each and every one of us aspire to be people who not only appreciate the church mothers, but also be appreciated and celebrated by them.

- The role of the pastor's wife as the "First Lady" is a part of the tradition of the church mothers. Even though the work is not found in the Bible, we can see and appreciate that many pastors' wives fill very important and essential roles within the church, and are due of the respect of being classified as an "elect lady" (2 John 1:1-6). They too are reminded of the importance of walking in love, loving others around them, and seeing themselves in positions of godly obedience.

REVIVING – AND RENEWING – CHURCH MOTHERS

While I have nothing against the concept of church mothers (obviously) I do believe that their image and function can use a bit of a make-over. Church mothers do not have to be people that uphold archaic principles and represent a bygone era. Here are some ways we can revive and renew church mothers to make their work more applicable in our modern time.

- **Stop forcing women into the pulpit** – As a female minister myself, this one might seem odd to many, but hear me out for a minute. I am not putting down women in ministry or saying in any way that women should not be in ministry. On the contrary, I think women belong in ministry and that arguments and debates about women not being in ministry are ridiculous. Now that having been said, I have noted a trend for the past few years where women are literally being shoved and forced to accept ministry positions. The implication is that if a woman takes anything less, she is somehow demeaning herself. We are told if a woman wants to participate in church, that must mean she is a preacher and she has to figure something out that relates to five-fold ministry. This is just as wrong as saying women have no place in ministry and can't preach or teach.

Why? Because ministry is something we are called to, not something that we should have to do as compulsory to our lives and understandings. If someone wants to be active in church and work with the younger women or men or just be involved in helps, then it's her right to do that. She should never feel like less or like what she is doing is unimportant. Church mothers started because women couldn't be in the pulpit, but they can also provide an important outlet for women who don't want to be in the pulpit because they don't feel called to be there. We need to make room for all of us in church, both those who are in ministry and those who are not, and make it all right for women to pursue occasional teaching and lots of helps or just supportive work and roles, as well.

- **Start a mentoring program** – There are plenty of people in the church who are older or retired who no longer have children at home and are looking for something constructive to do with their time. We know there is no end to the number of young church members who might need help in school, might like to learn an instrument or how to sing, or might be interested in helping young mothers with babysitting duties or household issues. Team up some older church members with some individuals who need help and mentoring.

- **Make sure your ministry of helps includes people of all ages** – The traditional idea of church mothers was seated in a section every Sunday in church, dressed to the nines. They might have been involved in some helps, but the general understanding was that the mothers were to be served. No matter what someone's age, everyone in the church should be involved in helps ministries, in volunteer projects at the church, and active participants and part of the community.

CHURCH MOTHERS IN HISTORY

While traditions rage on about female elders and the legitimacy of church mothers and first ladies, history has a long and rich tradition of female elders, the forerunners and rightful place of the church mother down through the centuries. Here are a few of them and the ground they broke for these women today.

- **Maris, Eulogius and Sobelus** – Mentioned in a letter attributed to Ignatius (although it is often considered incorrectly attributed), the women Mary, Eulogius and Sobelus were specifically appointed to serve in their community, believing that they were clearly fit to preside over the Word of God. They were considered to be positioned without doubt or question, and their positioning was quite important to the community at hand.[10]

- **Mercuria and Apollonia** – Even though we have no record of much about their lives or ministries, Dionysius of Alexandria (who died in 264) recounts two martyrs as "the most holy eldress Mecuria" and "a most remarkable virgin eldress Apollonia."[11]

- **Matthew's wife** – The Martyrdom of Matthew, which is an apocryphal document from the fourth or fifth century, speaks of the apostle Matthew ordaining his wife as a female elder. Even though many people reject the record and reject the role of women elders, it is obvious that a tradition of female elders existed in early church history.[12]

QUESTIONS AND ANSWERS

- **What is considered an appropriate age for a church mother?**

A female elder who is appointed to serve can be of any age if they are fit and prepared for service. A church mother, in the tradition that they typically serve, is usually considered an "older" woman. It is generally understood that church mothers are women who are past the age of raising their own families and are around the age of a grandmother. While there are no specified age limits or guidelines, I would say a church mother typically receives that sort of title around the time she turns fifty years of age.

- **Can a church mother be an ordained minister?**

Because being a church mother is more a position of honor and revere for life lived and the ability to assist and train up younger members of the church, I don't feel there is any reason why a woman of said age can't also be a minister. If a church mother is acknowledged as a female elder, she should be licensed as such. It is not typical, however, for church mothers (and first ladies) to be ordained.

- **Is it proper to call a First Lady "Mother?"**

In the Orthodox Church, the wives of priests are always referred to as "Mother." The role of the priest's wife is considered a hallowed and respectable one, comparable to our more modern role of the "First Lady." Their work in the church, however, is quite substantial. They are not just members who attend who are related to the priest, but take on an active role in shaping and forming the parish. I think that the propriety of calling a pastor's wife "mother" relates to her role and her activity in the faith and formation of a congregation, and how much she does. We know there are many pastors' wives who do extensive work and who are as involved in the church as any other staff member. There are those who simply attend the services as part of the pastor's family. It depends on the circumstance and on the relationship that you have with her as part of the faith community.

- **What role should church mothers and first ladies take in women's ministry?**

No matter what their specified role in the women's ministry may be, first ladies and church mothers should always participate in the work that is done among women in their congregation. I am not one who believes the pastor's wife always has to be in charge of all things women in the church, nor do I believe the church mothers have to assume that role all the time, either. I think having a women's minister in every church is essential, and overseeing the women's ministry is a part of that ministry responsibility. No matter how a church is structured, however, church mothers and first ladies should be a part of fellowship and services held specifically for women, because they are all women of the church.

- **Are church mothers and first ladies paid employees of a church?**

Since these are not ministerial positions, technically first ladies and church mothers are not paid employees of a church (unless they are somehow in ministry outside of their function or are ordained ministers of the organization).

- **Do church mothers have to dress a certain way?**

Church mothers should dress appropriately for services, as should everyone in church. As for a specific dress code, it is not typically mandated unless they are requested to wear a specific color suit (such as white or black) to designate them with honor during a special service.

DISCUSSION, STUDY AND REVIEW QUESTIONS

1. Why was the Apostle Paul's injunction for older women rather radical for his time? How did the Apostle Paul give them a purpose? How was this different from the rest of society?

2. What does the term "older women" or "aged women" actually refer to? How can we understand the work of the church mothers in this context? What does the Bible emphasize as important for these women?

3. Is the term "church mother" found in the Bible? What do we find instead in the New Testament? How are they to conduct themselves? How are they called to teach and encourage young men and women? How are they called to teach and encourage families? Whose footsteps do they follow in as women who pass on traditions of faith?

4. How do church mothers follow in the tradition of Eve? How do they magnify the relevance of being family in Christ? What opportunity does a church mother have within the church?

5. What value should church mothers always keep in mind? What happens when one is overly harsh or critical? Do people always have good relationships with their biological parents? How can church mothers help with this kind of a situation?

6. What does the work of a church mother center around? What happens when a woman is wise? What happens when a church mother is wise? How are church mothers always there for the Lord? Do they receive honor within their community? Why or why not?

7. What do church mothers remind us to be? Who gave the words of Proverbs 31 to King Lemuel? What does this tell us about her understanding? What should we, as people aspire to do and to be?

8. How is the role of the First Lady a part of the church mother tradition? What are they reminded to do, and why is it important for their function?

9. What are some ways we revive and renew the work of church mothers?

10. Who were some notable church mothers in history?

11. Discuss and share some of the questions and answers found in the "Questions and Answers" section. What did you learn that you did not know about church mothers? What did you learn that changed your mind about an opinion you might have had prior about church mothers? How did learning about specific issues related to church mothers help you to grow in your understanding of church mothers? The church? Your own relationship with God?

12. Who is your favorite church mother? Why are they your favorite?

Twelve ● MYSTIC

Theologians and other clerks,
You won't understand this book,
-- However bright your wits --
If you do not meet it humbly,
And in this way, Love and Faith
Make you surmount Reason, for
They are the protectors of Reason's house.
– Marguerite Porete[1]

PERHAPS the least understood function of all we have discussed in this book, I have saved it, with all its controversy, for last. The role of the mystic has been, ironically enough, veiled in shades of mystery for centuries. Misunderstanding its true purpose, we uphold the concept of the mystical without embracing its full depth and vision to change us and reveal the things we need to know as believers.

Because the mystical realm has both divine and demonic attributes and the two have been confused and confounded, the temptation has long existed for the church to throw out the entirety of mysticism, rather than truly sort through what is presented to it and discern the true from the false. In the Bible, all throughout church history, and in the deep and profound lives of many men and women, the work of the mystical experience is both real and powerful, undeniable, and yes, from God. While it might not make sense to our current understandings, while we might not always be able to understand its symbolism or see its relevance, the work of the mystic provides a powerful unveiling between the world that is unseen (the spiritual realm) and the realm that is seen (the natural world). Through experiential visions that are more than just visual, but incorporate all the senses, through perceptions, awareness, and tangibility, the mystic reminds us that God is real and all things spiritual are real, too, if we are but willing to receive the revelations for ourselves.

TEXT STUDY

2 Corinthians 12:1-10

POWER TEXTS

Isaiah 6:1-9, Ezekiel 1:1-2:10, Daniel 7:9-14, John 1:1-18, Luke 9:28-36, I Corinthians 1:18-25, I Corinthians 2:1-16, I Corinthians 3:16-23, Revelation 1:1-20, Revelation 4:1-11, Revelation 21:1-22:11.

KEY VERSE

2 Corinthians 12:3-4:

- *"And I knew such a man, (whether in the body, or out of the body, I cannot tell: God knoweth;) how that he was caught up to paradise, and heard unspeakable words, which it is not lawful for a man to utter."*

- *"And I know that this man – whether in the body or away from the body I do not know, God knows – was caught up into paradise, and he heard utterances beyond the power of man to put into words, which man is not permitted to utter."* (AMP)

- *"As I said, only God really knows if this man was in his body at the time. But he was taken up into paradise, where he heard things that are too wonderful to tell."* (CEV)

- *"I know that this person was snatched away to paradise where he heard things that can't be expressed in words, things that humans cannot put into words. I don't know whether this happened to him physically or spiritually. Only God knows."* (GW)

- *"I know that this man was caught up into paradise that he heard unspeakable words that were things no one is allowed to repeat. I don't know whether it was in the body or apart from the body. God knows."* (CEB)

- *"Yes, only God knows whether I was in my body or outside my body. But I do know that I was caught up to paradise and heard things so astounding that they cannot be expressed in words, things no human is allowed to tell."* (NLT)

POWER WORDS

- **Knew** – From the Greek word *eido* which means, "to see; to know."[2]

- **In body** – From two Greek words: *en* which means "in, by, with etc."[3] and *soma* which means "the body both of men or animals; the bodies of plants and of stars (heavenly bodies); is used of a (large or small) number of men closely united into one society, or family as it were; a social, ethical, mystical body; that which casts a shadow as distinguished from the shadow itself."[4]

- **Out of the body** – From two Greek words: *ektos* which means "outside, beyond; the outside, exterior; outside of;

beyond, besides, except"[5] and *soma* which means "the body both of men or animals; the bodies of plants and of stars (heavenly bodies); is used of a (large or small) number of men closely united into one society, or family as it were; a social, ethical, mystical body; that which casts a shadow as distinguished from the shadow itself."[6]

- **Caught up** – From the Greek word *harpazo* which means, "to seize, carry off by force; to seize on, claim for one's self eagerly; to snatch out or away."[7]

- **Paradise** – From the Greek word *paradeisos* which means "among the Persians a grand enclosure or preserve, hunting ground, park, shady and well watered, in which wild animals, were kept for the hunt; it was enclosed by walls and furnished with towers for the hunters; a garden, pleasure ground; the part of Hades which was thought by the later Jews to be the abode of the souls of pious until the resurrection: but some understand this to be a heavenly paradise; the upper regions of the heavens. According to the early church Fathers, the paradise in which our first parents dwelt before the fall still exists, neither on the earth or in the heavens, but above and beyond the world."[8]

- **Heard** – From the Greek word *akouo* which means, "to be endowed with the faculty of hearing, not deaf; to hear; to hear something."[9]

- **Unspeakable words** – From two Greek words: *arrhetos* which means "unsaid, unspoken; unspeakable (on account of its sacredness)"[10] and *rhema* which means "that which is or has been uttered by the living voice, thing spoken, word; subject matter of speech, thing spoken of."[11]

- **Lawful** – From the Greek word *exesti* which means "it is lawful."[12]

- **Utter** – From the Greek word *laleo* which means "to utter a voice or emit a sound; to speak; to talk; to utter, tell; to use words in order to declare one's mind and disclose one's thoughts."[13]

HISTORICAL CONTEXT

People have always been fascinated with the unseen spiritual world. Throughout the ages, people have always sought to see beyond the spiritual veil, peeking into the world beyond our immediate realm and understanding. To say that one had a mystical experience was a big deal, and often caused a lot of misunderstanding. Some people worshipped the individual who had a mystical experience, and many religions tried to inspire a mystical experience through what they perceived to be "hidden" knowledge. No matter how you want to spin it, the Apostle Paul clarifies that genuine mystical experience comes from God, many things about it are unexplainable, and that when you've had an experience like this, you can't deny it.

NOTES ON TEXT

The Apostle Paul's mystical experience lacks the specific details of what he experienced, but it does tell us that he was unsure of his physical state, he knows he was in paradise (the upper regions of heaven), he knew he went before the throne and heard powerful spiritual truths that he was unable to reiterate when he returned, and he knew that he had this experience by the power of God. This tells us that the mystical is not only possible, it is a realm that the mystic does experience. Even though it may be rare, it is very possible, and does happen.

POWER POINTS

- A mystic is an individual who has a mystical experience with God. Beyond just having a vision, a mystic does not just see what is to come, but they experience the full or nearly full sensory perception of the spiritual realm. In other words, they do not fully understand where they are; and they hear, smell, see, touch, and taste what they experience (2 Corinthians 12:1-10). The experience is beyond words and may be revealed in limitation (in the experience itself), in part (of only part of the revelation of a message) or in full (the message is delivered). Most mystical appearances appear to be limited or only revealed in part, as the full contents many are unable to understand or receive at the time the mystical experience occurs.

- Mystical experiences do not exist to puff up or to cause conceit (2 Corinthians 12:1-10, 1 Corinthians 3:16-23). They always have a purpose and a reason behind them, and it is always to reveal something beyond that which is physically seen. Above all things, the mystical experience proves God is real and proves that He is interested in us and He is working, even though we may not be able to see or understand how in the natural realm (Ezekiel 2:1-10).

- The mystic reminds us that God has the final say on all things we find clever, revealed, intelligent, or spiritual. No matter how wonderful we may esteem what we believe, everything that we believe is believed and taught "in part." We do not have the full revelation of all things that we will know after Jesus comes back, and the mystic gives us bits and shadows of that full revelation that is to come. Mysticism tells us clearly that God will destroy the wisdom of the wise, and that the foolish things of this world are exalted because of Him (1 Corinthians 1:18-25).

- The mystic also reminds us that God's wisdom is revealed to us by the Spirit, and that no natural eye has seen, no natural mind conceived, and no natural ear heard all that God has prepared for us. We like to talk about this verse in terms of natural things or gaining things, but God has spiritual things to reveal to us that are more important than natural things. The Spirit searches all things, including and especially the deep things of God, and the Spirit reveals them. Because we have the mind of Christ, we are able to embrace the things that seem as nonsense to the world, because the mystical reveals what has always been real, what is now real, and what will always be real, as well (2 Corinthians 2:1-16).

- Many mystical experiences overlap and contain similar elements. Many report seeing common elements from the throne room in heaven, the throne of God, the beings that surround the throne, the colors present in the spiritual realm, and the heavenly region (Isaiah 6:1-9, Ezekiel 1:1-28, Daniel 7:9-14, Revelation 4:1-11). Some also report having experiences of seeing and hearing from Christ, Who also is in heaven now (Revelation 1:1-20). We can clearly understand the entire book of Revelation to contain details of a mystical experience, partially revealed.

- The transfiguration of Jesus on the mount was a deeply mystical experience that Peter, James, and John were unable to speak about at the time they experienced it (Luke 9:28-36). Even though they knew they saw something incredible, unspeakable, and that showed forth powerful realities of what was to come through the work of Jesus and Who Jesus was, they were unable to reveal it until the proper time.

- The whole principle of Jesus as the Logos is deeply veiled in a mystical understanding. We do not often consider the intricacies of Jesus as the Logos, which we often translate as "word." Jesus' presence as the logos indicates God's order in creation and God's presence in the person of Christ. This indicates to us that the very presence of Jesus on the planet, His ministry, His sacrifice, and His work was all a part of a deeply mystical experience that God had with humanity (John 1:1-18). The light came into the world, amidst the darkness, and the darkness did not understand it. We still wrestle with those who do not see the powerful spiritual reality present in Jesus Christ, to this very day.

- Just as the book of Revelation contains an entire mystical experience (as was experienced by the Apostle John), the end chapters of Revelation reveal to us the true hope and vision God conveys to us through the long-term mystical revelation. It is His desire that we know He is real, that He desires us to know Him, and us to follow Him. The day and the hour promised in Revelation 21 and 22 are not just fantasies, but realities to come that are now revealed and prepared in heavenly places (Revelation 21:1-22:11). It is God's desire that we know Him in a deeper, more spiritual way, and the mystic brings that reality into full view, blocking out the many natural things that often blind our vision of divine truths.

DISCERNING MYSTICS

Not everyone who claims to be a mystic is sent from God. While there are many who claim to have visions and some who claim even more than that, the mystical realm does contain good and evil elements (which we know) and it is easy to be taken in by false experiences if we do not discern the true from the false. Here are a few ways we can discern through mystical experiences and come to a knowledge of what is for us and what is not.

- **They acknowledge evil does exist** – You would be amazed at the number of self-proclaimed mystics who walk away from their experiences claiming that there is nothing evil in the spiritual realm and everything is good. True mystics, as we can see from mystical experiences in the Bible, still maintain the balance of truth in their visions. They see both good and bad, and do not deny any true reality that is shown to them. Even if they do not have a vision of anything evil, they do not deny that such things exist. Mystics confirm and reveal what is true; they do not deny it or bring a counterfeit revelation.

- **They do not become arrogant** – An arrogant mystic is a false mystic. Attitude has a lot to do with confirming or denying the validity of a spiritual mystical experience. If someone comes back all full of themselves and the vision does not have a humbling effect, that pretty much indicates an individual has had a counterfeit vision.

- **They wrestle with the experience of what they have seen** – No matter how incredible a mystical vision might have been, a mystic will, most likely, deeply wrestle with the validity of what they have seen. They may doubt that what they experienced is real and they may find it difficult to talk about, especially at first. Even in one's life, when they may manifest the tangibility of the vision (in terms of feeling things in their physical being), they will still doubt or question what they have experienced. There are many mystics in history who never spoke of their experiences, choosing instead to journal on them. These works were not found or published until long after their death.

MYSTICS IN HISTORY

There are many known preachers and some preachers who were not as well-known. Take a look at four individuals you may or may not have heard of – and the work they did as preachers for the Lord.

- **Hadewijch (13th century)** – We have no details on the life of Hadewijch outside of her own writings. It appears she was the head of a Beguine house, and had Beguine influences. She most likely came from a privileged background and was well-educated. Her writings detail descriptions of her mystical experiences (written somewhere around the 1240s), as well as poetry and prose.[14]

- **Marguerite Porete (d. 1310)** – Another woman whose life we do not have any details on (outside of her heresy trial), Marguerite Porete was a French mystic who wrote *The Mirror of Simple Souls*, which addresses the ways that divine love works. She was associated with the Beguine movement, which was an order of Christian lay orders that lived semi-monastic, but worked as preachers and workers in practical matters in their time. The first version of her book seems to have been written in the 1290s, with it deemed heretical between 1296 and 1306. One of the reasons for this was that she wrote it in French instead of Latin, and it was to be burned and she was ordered not to write her ideas in a book again! Despite this command, she continued to write, and was arrested in 1308. She refused to speak during trial, and her works were examined and judged as heretical. Right up until the end, she was known for her calmness under pressure. Even though the book is not common today, it is known for its profound detailing based on mystical experience and is considered to be beautiful in its language, calling to union with God through perpetual joy and peace.[15]

- **Jakob Bohme (1575-1624)** – An influential German mystic, Jakob Bohme was raised in Lutheran tradition and grew up praying and reading the Bible. He experienced a number of mystical experiences as a child and seeing many spiritual truths in ordinary things. He tried hard to deny his experiences and focus instead on a career in shoemaking and having a family. He later began writing out his mystical experiences and, when they were deemed scandalous, he we would stop writing. With time, Jakob Boheme gained more strength and more insights, and wrote from a Protestant perspective (although it was not entirely Lutheran in its outlook) and remained within Christian tradition. He became important in many intellectual circles, and was taken very seriously in his mystical work.[16]

- **John Bunyan (Baptized 1628-1688)** – We do not know much about John Bunyan's early life, except to say that he had little school experience and was a part of the army during the English Civil War. His father and grandfather were involved in small homespun business work. We now know John Bunyan as the writer and preacher who wrote a religious allegory we call *The Pilgrim's Progress*. He converted to Christianity after getting married and working as a tinker for a time (following in his father's footsteps). He was first a Puritan, and then a member of the Bedford Free Church, a nonconformist group. He became a preacher and a writer. His views would land him in prison on at least two occasions, and while Incarcerated for twelve years, he had a spiritual experience that led him to write the allegory, *The Pilgrim's Progress*. Even though the writing was considered unpolished, it has remained a classic, down to the present day.[17]

QUESTIONS AND ANSWERS

- **Can a mystic experience physical symptoms (such as feeling or perceiving things related to the spiritual realm in their bodies)?**

I have heard of mystics having these experiences, especially because the mystical realm is very tangible to the senses. Not every mystic reports this kind of circumstance, but it is also not impossible.

- **Are mystics people we would consider to be "odd" or "unusual?"**

The labels "odd" or "unusual" tend to be subjective. It depends on how someone is viewing someone and through what perspective. In theory, anyone who is a true believer might be classified as strange to someone who is not, and many non-believers are classified as strange by believers. I do think, however, that people who have genuine mystical experiences do tend to be changed by them. They tend to be more preoccupied by spiritual matters and are not as interested in things that go on around them. They tend to notice and pick up on things that other people do not. For these reasons, someone might consider the workings of a mystic strange or unusual. I do not classify a true mystic as strange; I classify them as different.

- **How common are mystical experiences?**

Exact statistics on mystics and mysticism do not exist. There are countless in history who had these experiences and we know little to nothing about them. There are many more who never spoke up and took their experienced truths to the grave. It is my personal opinion that mystics are rare, and true, genuine mystical experiences, while they do happen, are not common everyday occurrences. We should all beware people who insist they have been to heaven dozens of times, claim to have seen all sorts of things, and brag on them as if they can and do happen to everyone.

- **If the Spirit is available to all, why aren't mystical experiences more common?**

Being a mystic is about more than just receiving the Spirit. While there is no question that the Spirit is available to all and that the Spirit pours out on all as He will, being a mystic or having a vision is not a part of the gifts of the Spirit. Because the role of the mystic is a church function, that means it happens as it is needed. It isn't something that is supposed to happen to everyone in the church, because not everyone can handle it. Mass mystical experiences would create confusion and chaos, and would isolate believers instead of drawing them together. While yes, many people would receive them, that would mean the understanding of them would not be present, and we could not receive the truths we need to from a mystical experience.

- **Is there anything someone can do to have a mystical experience?**

Mystical experiences are something an individual either has or does not have, and it is not something that can be manufactured by altered states of consciousness, using hallucinogenic drugs, or attempting to induce it by any stretch of the imagination.

- **Should mystics write what they experience?**

Sharing mystical experiences in written form is a long-standing means of preserving what has been seen. Even though most mystics remember the details of their experiences long after they have occurred, writing them down preserves the specific intricacies and messages that are to be conveyed. It was also a way to circulate the messages or teaching that they contained. I believe every mystic should write what they experience so subsequent generations can continue to learn from them.

DISCUSSION, STUDY AND REVIEW QUESTIONS

1. Have people always been fascinated with the spiritual world? Why do you think this is? What have people always sought to do throughout history? What was the response to a mystical experience in ancient times? What misunderstandings would come from mystical experiences? What does the Apostle Paul clarify about the mystical experience?

2. Even though the Apostle Paul's mystical experience lacks some details, what do we know about his experience? What does this tell us about mystical experiences?

3. What is a mystic? Do mystics just experience visions? What do they experience beyond a vision? Is the experience beyond words? How many possible ways are there to convey information about a mystical experience? How much do we receive about most mystical experiences?

4. Should a mystical experience cause conceit? Why or why not? What is the reason behind every mystical experience? What does the mystical exist to prove?

5. What does the mystic remind us about God? No matter how accurate we may believe our theories to be, how do we believe today? Do we have full revelation now? When will we have full revelation? What does mysticism clearly tell us God will do?

6. What else does the mystic remind us about the spiritual realm? What does the Spirit search? What are we able to understand? How does all of this relate to the mystical realm?

7. What similar elements do mystics report in their experiences? What kind of revelation was the book of Revelation?

8. What was a mystical experience had during the time of Jesus? Who experienced it? Why were they unable to reveal it at that time?

9. How does the revelation of Jesus as the Logos relate to mystical understanding?

10. What do the end chapters of the book of Revelation tell us? What does every mystical revelation hope we will discover? What do they tell and hope we will discern about God?

11. What are some ways we can discern mystics?

12. Who were some notable mystics in history?

13. Discuss and share some of the questions and answers found in the "Questions and Answers" section. What did you learn that you did not know about mystics? What did you learn that changed your mind about an opinion you might have had prior about mystics? How did learning about specific issues related to mystics help you to grow in your understanding of mystics? The church? Your own relationship with God?

14. Who is your favorite mystic? Why are they your favorite?

Thirteen ● OFFICES AND FUNCTIONS

But you, keep your head in all situations, endure hardship, do the work of an evangelist, discharge all the duties of your ministry.
- 2 Timothy 4:5 (NIV)

AS a conclusion to this book, we are going to spend this last chapter looking at the way the functions and the concept of functions assist and clarify issues within the five-fold ministry offices. Many who pursue ministry today experience confusion as to just what they are called to do. There are many reasons for this, but one of the main reasons for the confusion is because we do not properly understand the concept of a function. If we understand what a function is, it helps us to apply the principles of functions to the work of ministry and see that, many times over, ministers are operating in more functions than they might think.

Every minister has experienced times in ministry where they find themselves alone in a situation where they could use the input, gifts, and expertise of another minister. In fact, there are ministers who find themselves alone for more than just a situation. Sometimes when starting a ministry or a new work, we may not have access to the help we used to have. Even though our leaders and friends might be there for us, they might be in different regions or cities. Sometimes we visit an area to preach or on a missions trip and we can't call someone or have them come to help us. No matter what the circumstances might be, every minister has dealt with a situation where they are by themselves and their best apostle, or prophet, or evangelist, or pastor or teacher is not there with them and they have to go it alone.

The question becomes, what happens in this kind of situation? How does that minister, by themselves, handle whatever needs handling? We all know that in Christ, connection is important. It's easy to say reach out to someone where you are, but if you don't know anyone and are unsure of where you are, it is not that simple to do. There may also be other spiritual reasons why consultation with another minister with different gifts may not be an option.

Believe it or not, God has an answer to this sort of situation. Sometimes when we are in ministry, we might function in another office of the five-fold or even an appointment because we do not have the right support around us and, as a result, the benefits of having the full five-fold ministry within our reach is not always possible. This means that, for a time, God may give us the ability to do the work of another office or exercise their gifts in order to function in ministry, and the office we take on becomes a function in our lives. We may also pick up any one of the functions and start functioning in them. Understanding this helps explain why some people seem to have more than one ministry gift at a time, and how they properly are able to interact as ministers.

KEEP YOUR HEAD IN ALL SITUATIONS

Ministers of the Gospel must be prepared to encounter a variety of circumstances when they answer the call to ministry in the form of their five-fold ministry office. We have to trust that as we go through this walk, there will be thing we encounter that we don't know how to handle in the natural. Education and ministry training are important to help us avoid potential problems and pitfalls, but there will eventually be something in every minister's life and ministry work that they will be unprepared to handle.

This is where the functions come in, both the eleven we have discussed here in this book and the functional aspect of the five-fold ministry. When we don't know what to do, the Spirit inspires us to function in some way in order to handle that situation. Whether it's sending us a dream we can interpret ourselves, inspiring us to write, sending us a vision, or inspiring us to take on work that is a part of another five-fold ministry office, we are able to keep our head in each and every situation that comes along. By the leading of the Spirit, we are able to do what needs doing and know just what that is, even when we are unsure of it ourselves.

ENDURE HARDSHIP

If we understand the functions of the church to exist in response to need, then that tells us functions often exist in hardships. If we look at the Bible and we look at the history of ministry, gifts, and functions, they have often blossomed because of a difficult time or a hard time that brought about change and required such to stand up and be counted.

We don't like difficulty today, and I don't blame us for that one bit. Nobody likes feeling pressured or dealing with hard times. I have yet to meet a minister that enjoys the financial lack that too frequently comes with ministry, or the feeling of having to do so many things by yourself, especially at first. It's hard to endure hardship, to go through difficulties and not want to somehow avoid them.

I am sure God knows how hard it is for us to go through hardships, yet He doesn't let us out of them. He expects us not to avoid them, or skip them, or move around them, but to endure them. Have we ever considered that these parallel experiences come along for a reason? When we go through hardships, it forces us to function in different ways, both with offices and the functions of the church. God wants us to have different experiences in ministry, and hardship brings them out, every time.

DO THE WORK OF...

In the verse found at the beginning of this chapter, we are aware that the Apostle Paul told Timothy to "do the work of an evangelist." We've read this statement so many times, we don't think about what it means or what he was telling him to do. We have made it an evangelical command to preach the Gospel, which is correct. But what we need to see in this particular instance is something more that was being said to leadership in general. The Bible indicates Timothy was an apostle (Acts 19:22, I Thessalonians 1:1, I Thessalonians 2:6), not an evangelist. This means that, for whatever reason, the Apostle Paul was telling the Apostle Timothy to do a work – to do the work of the evangelist – or to function in that work. Now, notice what is said in the passage. Nowhere does it say that the Apostle Timothy was an evangelist. It does not say he became an Apostle-Evangelist, nor does it say he took off the apostolic call on his life. What the Apostle Paul was telling the Apostle Timothy to do was simple: he was telling him to function as an evangelist. He was telling him that for this point in his ministry, he needed to be about the business of spreading the Gospel and to take on the work of the evangelist as a function.

It is perfectly possible for a minister of the five-fold to take on any other office of the five-fold ministry as a function, just as the Apostle Paul told the Apostle Timothy to function as an evangelist. It is possible to do the work of any of the offices and not specifically be one of those other offices, out of need, for a period of time. This is one of the ways that the Spirit moves through the Body, ensuring that every need is met as it arises.

DISCHARGE ALL THE DUTIES OF YOUR MINISTRY

If we look at many of the different things that go into a ministry call, there are many duties that overlap. All the ministers of the five-fold are supposed to engage people with the Gospel, all of them involve the ability to be inter-personal, and in modern times, every minister has certain legal and administrative duties in order to execute a ministry within the bounds of the law and keeping things decent and in order. This means that as we discharge, we need the added bonus of the functions to keep us going and keep things tight and neat as we go forth with the Gospel.

A FINAL THOUGHT ABOUT FUNCTIONS

God has given us an incredible gift in the functions of the church and in the function of ministers through the five-fold ministry. It is a wonderful thing to be a part of the Body of Christ and watch Him work. It is an even more wonderful thing to be active in the church. For centuries, many church members have taken a back seat to church and left everything up to ministers. The spiritual gifts of the church and the functions of the church remind us that church is for participation. Ministers are reminded that church is not static and ministry is not one-sided, but multi-faceted. God has given us everything that we need, if we will only rely on the Spirit to guide and direct us. The Spirit is there. The ministry is real. The functions are real. The gifts are real. The appointments are real. Now we need to believe the Spirit is there, for real, and not on a long-lost retirement or vacation. Now is the time to embrace the fullness of faith that God has for each and every one of us so the church can fully function.

References

CHAPTER 2

[1]"Roll Jordan Roll." http://sites.duke.edu/blackatlantic/2014/03/18/roll-jordan-roll-a-community-in-song-and-sound/. Accessed on June 29, 2015.
[2]*Strong's Exhaustive Concordance of the Bible*, #4198
[3]Ibid., #537
[4]Ibid., #2889
[5]Ibid., #2784
[6]Ibid., #2098
[7]Ibid., #3956
[8]Ibid., #2937
[9]"George Whitefield." https://en.wikipedia.org/wiki/George_Whitefield. Accessed on June 30, 2015.
[10]"Zilpha Elaw." https://en.wikipedia.org/wiki/Zilpha_Elaw. Accessed on June 30, 2015.
[11]"Women in Religion." http://www.seeking4truth.com/women_in_religion.htm. Accessed on June 30, 2015.

CHAPTER 3

[1]"Missionary Quotes." http://www.goodreads.com/quotes/tag/missionary?page=2. Accessed on June 30, 2015.
[2]*Strong's Exhaustive Concordance of the Bible*, # 3212
[3]Ibid., #3548
[4]Ibid., #3427
[5]Ibid., #3384
[6]Ibid., #4941
[7]Ibid., #3372
[8]Ibid., #3068

[9]"Alopen." https://en.wikipedia.org/wiki/Alopen. Accessed July 2, 2015.
[10]"William Carey (Missionary)." https://en.wikipedia.org/wiki/William_Carey_%28missionary%29. Accessed July 2, 2015.
[11]"Betsey Stockton." https://en.wikipedia.org/wiki/Betsey_Stockton. Accessed July 2, 2015.
[12]"Gladys Aylward." https://en.wikipedia.org/wiki/Gladys_Aylward. Accessed July 2, 2015.
[13]"Top 10 Most Dangerous Countries for Christians." http://listverse.com/2011/11/24/top-10-most-dangerous-countries-for-christians/. Accessed July 2, 2015.
[14]"The Surprising Countries Most Missionaries Are Sent From And Go To." http://www.christianitytoday.com/gleanings/2013/july/missionaries-countries-sent-received-csgc-gordon-conwell.html. Accessed July 2, 2015.

CHAPTER 4

[1]"Visionary Quotes." http://thinkexist.com/quotes/with/keyword/visionaries/. Accessed on July 2, 2015.
[2]*Strong's Exhaustive Concordance of the Bible*, #2078
[3]Ibid., #2250
[4]Ibid., #1632
[5]Ibid., #4151
[6]Ibid., #3956
[7]Ibid., #4561
[8]Ibid., # 5207
[9]Ibid., #2364
[10]Ibid., #4395
[11]Ibid., #3495
[12]Ibid., #3706
[13]Ibid., #4245
[14]Ibid., #1797
[15]"Perpetua and Felicity." https://en.wikipedia.org/wiki/Perpetua_and_Felicity. Accessed on July 3, 2015.
[16]"Catherine of Siena." https://en.wikipedia.org/wiki/Catherine_of_Siena. Accessed on July 3, 2015.
[17]"Martin Luther." https://en.wikipedia.org/wiki/Martin_Luther. Accessed on July 3, 2015.
[18]"John Bosco." http://www.catholic.org/saints/saint.php?saint_id=63. Accessed on July 4, 2015.

CHAPTER 5

[1]"Dreams Quotes." http://www.notable-quotes.com/d/dreams_quotes.html. Accessed on July 6, 2015.
[2]*Strong's Exhaustive Concordance of the Bible*, # 3493
[3]Ibid., #7308

[4]Ibid., #4486
[5]Ibid., #7924
[6]Ibid., #6590
[7]Ibid., #2493
[8]Ibid., #0263
[9]Ibid., #0280
[10]Ibid., #8271
[11]Ibid., #7001
[12]Ibid., #7912
[13]Ibid., #1841
[14]Ibid., #1096
[15]Ibid., #6591

CHAPTER 6
[1]"Quotes About Intercession."
https://www.goodreads.com/quotes/tag/intercession. Accessed on July 6, 2015.
[2]*Strong's Exhaustive Concordance of the Bible*, #3870
[3]Ibid., #4412
[4]Ibid., #1162
[5]Ibid., #4335
[6]Ibid., #1783
[7]Ibid., #2169
[8]Ibid., #3956
[9]Ibid., #444
[10]Ibid., #935
[11]Ibid., #5247
[12]Ibid., #2263
[13]Ibid., #2272
[14]Ibid., #979
[15]Ibid., #2150
[16]Ibid., #4587
[17]"Gertrude The Great." https://en.wikipedia.org/wiki/Gertrude_the_Great. Accessed on July 8, 2015.
[18]"Andrew Murray." https://en.wikipedia.org/wiki/Andrew_Murray_(minister). Accessed on July 8, 2015.
[19]"Corrie ten Boom." https://en.wikipedia.org/wiki/Corrie_ten_Boom. Accessed on July 7, 2015.
[20]"Watchman Nee." https://en.wikipedia.org/wiki/Watchman_Nee. Accessed on July 8, 2015.

CHAPTER 7

[1]"Gates, Watchmen, Gatekeepers, and Walls."
http://creatingnewworlds.org/2012/10/13/gates-watchmen-gatekeepers-and-walls/. Written on October 13, 2012. Accessed on July 8, 2015.

[2]Strong's Exhaustive Concordance of the Bible, # 6822

[3]Ibid., #7323

[4]Ibid., #7121

[5]Ibid., #7778

[6]Ibid., #1319

[7]"St. Alexander Akimetes."
http://www.catholic.org/saints/saint.php?saint_id=1240. Accessed on July 8, 2015.

[8]"Leoba." https://en.wikipedia.org/wiki/Leoba. Accessed on July 8, 2015.

[9]"Olga of Kiev." https://en.wikipedia.org/wiki/Olga_of_Kiev. Accessed on July 8, 2015.

[10]"Rees Howells." https://en.wikipedia.org/wiki/Rees_Howells. Accessed on July 8, 2015.

CHAPTER 8

[1]"Quotes about service." http://www.goodreads.com/quotes/tag/service. Accessed on July 9, 2015.

[2]Strong's Exhaustive Concordance of the Bible, # 1401

[3]Ibid., #1399

[4]Ibid., #1632

[5]Ibid., #2250

[6]Ibid., #4151

[7]Ibid., #4395

[8]"Philip Neri." https://en.wikipedia.org/wiki/Philip_Neri. Accessed on July 9, 2015.

[9]"Titus Coan." https://en.wikipedia.org/wiki/Titus_Coan. Accessed on July 9, 2015.

[10] "Evangeline Booth." https://en.wikipedia.org/wiki/Evangeline_Booth. Accessed on July 9, 2015.

[11] "Ida S. Scudder." https://en.wikipedia.org/wiki/Ida_S._Scudder. Accessed on July 9, 2015.

CHAPTER 9

[1]"Quotations About Writing." http://www.quotegarden.com/writing.html. Accessed on July 9, 2015.

[2]Strong's Exhaustive Concordance of the Bible, #3414

[3]Ibid., #4039

[4]Ibid., #1263

[5]Ibid., #5608

[6]Ibid., #5374

[7]Ibid., #3789

[8]Ibid., #6310

[9]Ibid., #5612

[10]Ibid., #3079

[11]Ibid., #8313

[12]Ibid., #3254

[13]Ibid., #1697

[14]"William Tyndale." https://en.wikipedia.org/wiki/William_Tyndale. Accessed on July 11, 2015.

[15]"John Foxe." https://en.wikipedia.org/wiki/John_Foxe. Accessed on July 11, 2015.

[16]"Anne Dutton." https://en.wikipedia.org/wiki/Anne_Dutton. Accessed on July 11, 2015.

[17]"Sarah Osborn." https://en.wikipedia.org/wiki/Sarah_Osborn. Accessed on July 11, 2015.

CHAPTER 10

[1]"Words of Wisdom – Parenting and Education." http://www.trans4mind.com/quotes/quotes-parenting-education.html. Accessed on July 11, 2015.

[2]*Strong's Exhaustive Concordance of the Bible*, # 3463

[3]Ibid., #3807

[4]Ibid., #3962

[5]Ibid., #1080

[6]Ibid., #2098

[7]"Desert Fathers." https://en.wikipedia.org/wiki/Desert_Fathers. Accessed on July 11, 2015.

[8]"Desert Mothers." https://en.wikipedia.org/wiki/Desert_Mothers. Accessed on July 11, 2015.

[9]"Saint Savvas the Spiritual Father of Ioannina." http://www.johnsanidopoulos.com/2015/02/saint-savvas-spiritual-father-of.html. Accessed on July 11, 2015.

[10]"Susanna Wesley." https://en.wikipedia.org/wiki/Susanna_Wesley. Accessed on July 11, 2015.

CHAPTER 11

[1]"Mother's Day Church Sign Sayings." http://www.sayingsforchurchsigns.com/freeresource/mothers-day/. Accessed on July 12, 2015.

[3]Ibid., #2688

[4]Ibid., #2412
[5]Ibid., #1228
[6]Ibid., #1402
[7]Ibid., #4183
[8]Ibid., #3631
[9]Ibid, #2567
[10]"The Neglected History Of Women In The Early Church."
https://www.christianhistoryinstitute.org/magazine/article/women-in-the-early-church/. Accessed on July 12, 2015.
[11]Ibid.
[12]Ibid.

CHAPTER 12

[1]"Quotes about Mystics." https://www.goodreads.com/quotes/tag/mystic. Accessed on July 12, 2015.
[2]*Strong's Exhaustive Concordance of the Bible*, #1492
[3]Ibid., #1722
[4]Ibid., #4983
[5]Ibid., #1622
[6]Ibid., #4983
[7]Ibid., #726
[8]Ibid., #3857
[9]Ibid., #191
[10]Ibid., #731
[11]Ibid., #4487
[12]Ibid., #1832
[13]Ibid., #2980
[14]"Hadewijch." https://en.wikipedia.org/wiki/Hadewijch. Accessed on July 13, 2015.
[15]"Marguerite Porete." https://en.wikipedia.org/wiki/Marguerite_Porete. Accessed on July 13, 2015.
[16]"Jakob Bohme." https://en.wikipedia.org/wiki/Jakob_B%C3%B6hme. Accessed on July 13, 2015.
[17] "John Bunyan." https://en.wikipedia.org/wiki/John_Bunyan. Accessed on July 13, 2015.

● About the Author

DR. LEE ANN B. MARINO, PH.D., D. MIN, D.D.

These that have turned the world upside down are come hither also.
- Acts 17:6

DR. **LEE ANN B. MARINO, PH.D., D.MIN., D.D.** is an apostle, missionary, apostolic theologian, Bible scholar, women's advocate, feminist, activist, university chancellor, songwriter, worship leader, worship dancer, and Senior Prelate, founder, and visionary for Apostolic Fellowship International Revival Ministries (AFIRM). In acknowledgement of her extensive work in the apostolic, she has been called "the greatest apostle in the modern church." A seminary doctoral graduate of Apostolic Preachers College (now Apostolic University) in Philosophy, Theology, Divinity, and Religion/Comparative Religion, Dr. Marino's approach to preaching, teaching, Spiritual matters, and Scriptural education have touched a generation looking for leadership, connection, and understanding in our modern times.

In nearly two decades of ministry, Dr. Marino has made the joke that she's been "every Pentecostal denomination under the sun." A college exploration of religion back in 1997 led her to "get saved the first time," immersing her into a spiritual world of gifts, devotional spirituality, and an intense call to ministry, sometimes in churches that worked – and sometimes in settings that went seriously awry. Through a series of different events, including periods of time in Charismatic, Holiness, Full Gospel, Oneness, Apostolic, and non-denominational, Dr. Marino found her own calling – and her own ministerial identity – in neo-Apostolic, a division of modern Pentecostal understanding that respects and heralds the ancestry of the past, along with vision for the modern-day issues and circumstances the church and the world face today.

Dr. Marino has been in ministry since 1998 and founded Apostolic Fellowship International Ministries (now Apostolic Fellowship International Revival Ministries) in 2004. She was ordained as a pastor in 2002 and as an apostle in 2010. Her experiences have taken her to over five hundred religious services and experiences of all sorts throughout the years, both Christian and non-Christian alike, as she studied and strived to learn what all believe. The work of Apostolic Fellowship International Revival Ministries now extends to all Christian borders, working in different Protestant and non-denominational churches alike. Apostle's vision is about the church now, honoring history while looking forward, and about becoming "all things to all people," that some may be saved. Her fellowship encompasses twenty churches and ministries worldwide, thousands of friends, and includes the work of Sanctuary International Fellowship Tabernacle – SIFT, a church movement dedicated to leading people to God without politics, where she emphasizes relationship, acceptance, experience, and service. In covering, her emphasis is on the unique development of each leader to become all God has for them to be in their specific gifting and ministries. She has preached and taught throughout the United States, Puerto Rico, and in Europe. Affectionately nicknamed "the Spitfire," she is best-known for her work in the apostolic, her instruction for church leaders and ministers, her work in the study of gender, sexual ethics, and human sexuality, and her work in women's ministry through the study of Female Apologetics, established and first taught by Dr. Marino herself. She has spent over twenty years in advocacy, education, and work for and with minority communities, including women, African-Americans, Latinos, and the LGBT community.

Her work is not without acclaim, and she is the recipient of several awards and has been featured in many magazine publications and on many radio and television programs over the years, including Woman of the Year 2012 and Mother of the Year 2013. As Chancellor of Apostolic University since 2004, her teachings in the apostolic, church history and protocol, Scripture studies, textbooks, and educational materials on many issues of faith, ethics, gender, sociology, church history, theology, and philosophy have reached individuals in over seventy-five countries. Having written over twenty-five books, including her best-sellers, *Ministry School Boot Camp: Training For Helps Ministries, Appointments, And Beyond* (Righteous Pen Publications, 2014), *Awakening Christian Ministry: The Call To Serve Others As We Serve Jesus Christ* (Righteous Pen Publications, 2014), *Stumbling To Nineveh: A Journey Through The Book Of Jonah* (Righteous Pen Publications, 2015); *Discovering Intimacy: A Journey Through The Song Of Solomon* (Righteous Pen Publications, 2015); and *Ministering To LGBTs – And Those Who Love Them* (Apostolic University Press, 2016).

Dr. Marino is editor-in-chief of *Kingdom Now* Magazine and host of the *Kingdom Now* television and radio programs, as well as CEO and designer for Rose of Sharon Creations, CEO of Righteous Pen Media, and Editor-in-Chief for The Righteous Pen Publications Group. She is also a member of the Women's Christian Temperance Union, a historical women's organization with long-held ties to women's rights, ordination, and ministry. Her main website is www.kingdompowernow.org.